# experience the
# power of history

T hree thousand years of history brought vividly to life in five magnificent themed galleries. Come face to face with the past as eight thousand permanent exhibits transport you on a journey through time.

An endless choice of things to see and do inside and outside including live dramatic interpretations, handling collections, interactives, horse-riding, falconry displays and an ever changing events programme.

All in all, a fun filled, enjoyable and inspiring day out for the entire family.

FREE
MUSEUM
ENTRY

## ROYAL ARMOURIES MUSEUM

Armouries Drive, Leeds, LS10 1LT, 24 hour Information Line: 0113 220 1999
Website: www.armouries.org.uk  Email: enquiries@armouries.org.uk

## Welcome to the first edition of the Leeds Guide Kids' Guide!

We hope that you are as impressed and inspired by the number and range of attractions in the region as we were when we compiled this book. Yorkshire is blessed with both vibrant urban areas and beautiful countryside: each provides a wealth of things to do and places to go, from spectacular, well-known favourites to fascinating hidden corners, with something to suit every pocket and type of family.

If you enjoy visiting the places in this guide, be sure to catch up on more of what's happening in The Leeds Guide: we provide up-to-date listings, previews and features on events in the region and have a special section devoted to kids' items. It's available from your newsagent every fortnight.

Finally, we shall be producing a second Kids' Guide for 2004-5: feel free to write in with your suggestions for improvements, places that we have missed or any that do not provide the facilities listed in this volume. We would like it to reflect the experiences of you and your children, as we too are looking forward to seeing the Kids' Guide grow in coming years.

## Contacts

Published annually by
**Leeds Guide Ltd, 30-34 Aire Street, Leeds LS1 4HT**
Tel 0113 244 1000  Fax 0113 244 1002
www.leedsguide.co.uk

| | |
|---|---|
| **Editorial** | 0113 244 1007 |
| | editor@leedsguide.co.uk |
| **Advertising** | 0113 244 1005 |
| | sales@leedsguide.co.uk |
| **Design** | 0113 244 8484 |
| | design@leedsguide.co.uk |

**Editor** Abi Bliss
**Contributors** Abi Bliss, Laurence Boyce, Laura Cross, Hazel Davis, Dom Dwight, Belinda Green, Dan Jeffrey, Rich Jevons, Richard Redwin, Anna Stewart
**Photography** Chris Kell, Krit Kritmanorote
**Cover Photo:** © Miep van Damm / Masterfile

**Managing Director** Bruce Hartley
**Publishing Director** Bill Graham
**Sales Executives** Ian Macdonald and Matt Hamilton
**Design** Blueprint Design 0113 244 8484
Romilly Bean, Lenka Hulmes, David Donaghy
**Printers** Buxton Press
**Distribution** John Menzies UK Ltd

Published annually in July. Although every effort has been made to ensure the accuracy of the information contained in this publication, Leeds Guide Ltd cannot accept responsibility for any errors it may contain. Leeds Guide Ltd cannot be held responsible for the loss or damage of any material, solicited or unsolicited. No reproduction of any part of this publication, in any form or by any means, without prior written consent from Leeds Guide Ltd. The views expressed in this publication do not necessarily reflect those of the advertisers or the publishers. ©Leeds Guide Ltd 2003  ISBN 0-9544641-2-5

**LEEDS GUIDE**

## How to use the guide

The guide is broken down into nine main sections: Museums and Places to Visit; Parks, Farms and Railways; Shopping; Theatres, Cinemas and Concerts; Eating and Drinking; Clubs, Societies and Workshops; Sport; Parties and Playtime and Days Out.

These main sections contain smaller sub-categories: for example, Museums and Places to Visit covers not only museums but also attractions such as theme parks, with subsections on galleries, and houses and castles. Eating and Drinking highlights restaurants which welcome children and either provide them with a special menu or portions suited to kid-sized appetites, whilst Parties and Playtime lists places where you could book a birthday party, entertainers such as magicians and special play venues for kids. Days Out suggests places either inside the region or within easy travelling distance that merit more than a passing visit — to help, we have included maps and public transport information for the area. Finally, there is a quick reference calendar to give you an idea of some of the events worth catching over the next year.

Wherever possible a listing for an attraction or organisation will include the address and phone number. These are followed by (where applicable) opening days/times and prices, information on age suitability and capacity (eg for party venues) and, for restaurants, a list of child-friendly facilities such as whether the venue offers a highchair.

sponsored by
**ROYAL ARMOURIES MUSEUM**

# Colourful characters

# Magical setting

There's a lot to enjoy at Harewood. The House itself, with exquisite Adam interiors, Chippendale furniture and outstanding art collections. A thousand acres of glorious Grounds and Gardens, with an Adventure Playground that children love. The lakeside Bird Garden with around 100 exotic species. Plus an exciting programme of exhibitions and special events throughout the season. It's a magical setting you'll want to revisit.

## HAREWOOD

**VISITOR ATTRACTION OF THE YEAR**
*WHITE ROSE AWARDS 2002*

**Seven miles from Leeds and Harrogate on the A61.**
**Open daily from 26 March to 2 November 2003.**
For information telephone (0113) 218 1010, or visit our website www.harewood.org

Designated as a museum with an outstanding collection

Registered Charity No. 517753 Harewood House is a charitable educational trust, set up to maintain and develop Harewood, its collections and grounds, for the public benefit.

Museums & Places to Visit

Lightwater Valley

## Museums and Places to Visit

Yorkshire has masses of places for kids to visit, from high-profile institutions such as the NMPFT and Eureka! to smaller treasures such as Ilkley Toy Museum. Nowdays most museums have transformed themselves from the dusty display cabinets of yore and as such many of these establishments occupy a middle ground between education and pure entertainment: think of the 'time capsules' at the Jorvik Viking museum as a slower (and smellier) version of Lightwater Valley's high-octane thrills and spills. Even places such as art galleries and stately homes which used to recoil in horror at the prospect of a visitation of little, sticky hands have programmes and exhibitions designed specially for children. Many of these attractions are free or offer reasonable family deals — however, kids and adults alike may find it hard to resist the charms of the ubiquitous gift shop.

### Abbey House Museum
Revisit Victorian Leeds, with galleries, events, monthly activities and perfectly reconstructed old shops
*Abbey Walk, Leeds • 0113 275 5821 • Open Tue-Fri and Sun 10am-5pm, Sat 12-5pm • Adults £3, Students £2, OAP £2, Children £1, Family ticket £5*

### Armley Mills Industrial Museum
See Jack, the museum's 100-year old steam locomotive and go back in time to when Leeds was a small market town and discover about life during the Industrial Revolution.
*Canal Road, Armley, Leeds • 0113 263 7861 • Open Tue-Sat 10am-5pm, Sun 1pm-5pm • Children 50p, Adults £2, Students £1, OAP £1*

Armley Mills

### Bagshaw Museum
Museum dedicated to its founders the Bagshaw family and their travels throughout Asia, Africa and the Americas, displaying artefacts from all the far-flung places they travelled. Children can see inside a recreated tomb interior in the Kingdom of Osiris Gallery as well as discover all about tropical rain forests in the Enchanted Forest. There are also exhibitions of local history as well as a gift shop representing the exotic travels of the family.
*Wilton Park, Batley, Batley • 01924 326 155 • Open Mon-Fri 11am-5pm, Sat-Sun 12-5pm • Adults £2, OAP £1, Students £1, Children 50p*

### Bankfield Museum
Impressive Italianate mansion overlooking the Halifax village of Ackroyden and containing an internationally renowned textile and costume collection, including textiles from Eastern Europe, mummy wrappings, woven cloth from Africa and a Diaghilev costume. As well as the Duke of Wellington's Regimental Museum, containing the original Wellington boots, there are all year round workshops, masterclasses and demonstrations.
*Boothtown Road, Halifax • 01422 354 823 • Open Wed-Sun 12pm-5pm • Free*

### Bolling Hall Museum
Medieval hall furnished according to selected eras from the last 500 years. Children can see how a 17th-century kitchen operated, how 16th-century ladies passed the time and gaze at the intricately carved furniture. There are large gardens in which to picnic as well as a shop and baby changing area.
*Bolling Hall Road, Bradford • 01274 723057 • Open Wed-Fri 11am-4pm, Sat 10-5pm, Sun 12-5pm. • Free*

### Bracken Hall Countryside Centre
Centre and garden housing displays relating to the natural history, geology, archaeology and local history of the area. The garden has all the features of an everyday garden, demonstrating to children how they too can cultivate wildlife at home. There is also a programme of guided walks and events throughout the year.
*Glen Road, Baildon, Shipley • 01274 584 140 • Open 12pm-5pm • Free*

### Bradford Industrial Museum
Experience life through the ages in Bradford with a variety of activities including recreations of Victorian classrooms (with full costume), emigration workshops, old-fashioned washdays and life in Bradford during the Second World War. There are also appearances from the museum's own theatre group, 'Flying Shuttles' who present a series of plays in different areas of the

museum. Indoor/outdoor eating, café, shop, baby changing facilities.
*Moorside Mills, Eccleshill, Bradford • 01274 435900 • Open Tues-Sat 10am-5pm, Sun 12-5pm • Free*

### Bronte Birthplace
'The Bethlehem of the Bronte World'. Birthplace of the famous Bronte sisters, and the house in which the family lived from 1815 to 1820. Writers Barbara Whitehead and Bernard Mayston are gradually restoring the interior to the Regency period.
*72/74 Market Street, Thornton, Bradford • 01274 830 849 • Open Apr-Sep: Sun, Tues and Bank Holiday Mon 12-4pm • Adults £3, Children £1.50*

### Bronte Parsonage Museum
Perhaps a little dull for many children's tastes, the Bronte Parsonage Museum is nonetheless a fascinating exhibition of an extraordinary family and the era and area in which they lived. See costumes, handwriting excerpts and personal memorabilia from the Brontes as well as local historical artefacts and pictures.
*Haworth, Keighley • 01535 640194 • Open Apr-Sep daily 10am-5.30pm, Oct-Mar daily 11am-5pm with exceptions in Jan and Feb • Adults £4.80, Children £1.50, Students £3.50, OAP £3.50*

### Burnby Hall Gardens & Museum
Home to more varieties of lily (in their natural habitat) than anywhere else in Europe, Burnby Hall Gardens and Museum also play host to a large amount of ornamental trees, shrubs, fish and birds, all of which you can feed with special food available on entry. The gardens also act as a venue for summer concerts and the museum situated within the grounds contains memorabilia from the travels of Major Stewart who founded the gardens. There is a gift shop and tea rooms also located within the grounds.
*Pocklington, York • 01759 302 068 • Open 10am-5pm • Adults £2.70, Children £1.20, OAP £2.20*

### Cartwright Hall
Bradford's main art gallery, situated in the extensive grounds of Lister Park, contains Victorian and Edwardian art as well as important twentieth century collections. The museum runs year-round educational projects including events to promote the enjoyment of drawing and digital photography. There is also a new Transcultural Gallery containing South Asian art and artefacts.
*Lister Park, Bradford • 01274 751 212 • Open Tue-Sat and Bank Holiday Mon 10am-5pm, Sun 1-5pm • Free*

**be amazed...**
Experience the past, present and future of photography, film and television with amazing interactive displays and spectacular 3D IMAX cinema.

Museum admission is **FREE**

**experience**

**understand**

THE NATIONAL MUSEUM OF PHOTOGRAPHY, FILM & TELEVISION, BRADFORD, BD1 1NQ
Box Office: 0870 70 10 200
www.nmpft.org.uk

# Museums & Places to Visit

Courtesy of Bradford Council

Colour Museum

history of textile colouring. There are also half-day workshops for children of all ages on anything from dyeing and stained glass making to coats of arms and mask making.
*Providence Street, Off Westgate, Bradford • 01274 390955 • Open Tue-Sat 10am-4pm. Adults £2, children £1.50. • Adults £1.50, Children £1, Family ticket £3.75*

## Courthouse Museum
Featured as Ashfordly Magistrates Court by Yorkshire Television for scenes in 'Heartbeat'. The former Ripon Liberty Courthouse closed as a working courthouse in 1998 and opened as a living museum where visitors can stand in the dock where prisoners were sentenced to transportation to Australia, learn about the Proclamation of Vice and watch an audio visual presentation of the re-enactment of cases heard during its opening week in 1830.
*Minster Road, Ripon, North Yorkshire • 01765 602 133 • Open 1 Apr-26 Oct daily 1-4pm except 1 Jul-31 Aug daily 11am-4pm • Adults £1; Children Free*

## Dales Countryside Museum
The displays and hands-on exhibits tell the story of the Yorkshire Dales landscape and people over the last 10,000 years. Children can experience the Time Tunnel where they can see and examine unique exhibits from the Stone Age to Victorian times or take a trip on the static train and find out how much family life has changed in the Dales. There is also a 'lead mine' where you can discover how the various industries of the area have helped to make it what it is today. The museum holds regular events, demonstrations of traditional crafts and changing exhibitions.
*Station Yard, Hawes, North Yorkshire • 01969 667 450 • Open Daily • Adults £3, Children Free*

## Clarke Hall
A late 17th-century farmer's house and gardens, fully preserved and open to school and community groups during term time, holding 'living history' open days as well as public events.
*Aberford Road, Wakefield • 01924 302 700 • Open Tue-Thu 11am-3.30pm • Adults £3.50, Children Free*

## Cliffe Castle Museum
Displays of local fossils, minerals and geological artefacts; stained glass and pottery and Victorian furnishings. Outside there's aviaries and a kids' play area.
*Spring Gardens Lane, Keighley • 01535 618 230 • Open Tues-Sat and Bank Holiday Mon 10am-5pm, Sun 12-5pm. • Free*

## Colne Valley Museum
Independent museum housed in three weavers' cottages and displaying memorabilia associated with local life and industry from 1840-1920. There are two livings rooms, a loom chamber with two looms, a spinning jenny, cropping display, a gas lit cloggers shop and a room devoted to a series of exhibitions which are changed every six weeks. There are also craft demonstrations most weekends.
*Cliffe Ash, Golcar, Huddersfield • 01484 659762 • Open Sat, Sun and Bank Holidays 2-5pm • Adults £1.10, Children 55p*

## Colour Museum
Britain's only museum dedicated to the study of colour. There are two main galleries; The World of Colour and Colour and Textiles, each one containing hands-on exhibits and demonstrations including the mixing of coloured light, colour through animals' eyes and the

## Dewsbury Museum
Museum charting the changing face of childhood over the last two centuries in a reconstructed 1940s classroom with an exhibition of antique toys and playthings.
*Wilton Park, Batley, West Yorkshire • 01924 326 155 • Open Mon-Fri 11am-5pm, Sat-Sun 12-5pm • Free*

## Earth Centre
Centre of sustainable development in everyday life, consisting of wetland with wildlife, terraced gardens, indoor and outdoor exhibitions including sensory walks, a waterworks exhibition and many outdoor and indoor activities including abseiling, zip wire, archery and craft workshops as well as regular 'bike weekends'. For younger children there is Bluebeard's Play Galleon and for exhausted parents Shipwreck Island Adventure Golf.

Denaby Main, Doncaster • 01709 512 000 • Open 10am-5pm • Adults £4.50, Children £3.50, Students £3.50

### Eden Camp

Modern history theme museum where you can experience the sounds and smells of wartime Britain, relive civilian life and see informative exhibits and displays.

Malton, Ryedale, North Yorkshire • 01653 697 777 • Open 10am to 5pm, last admission 4pm • Adults £4, Children £3

### Eureka!

Halifax's very own museum for children is a national phenomenon. It boasts over 400 different hands-on exhibits — ranging from the scientific to the creative as well as regular workshops on everything from gardening to acting — which are only accessible to small people (it's a much bemoaned fact that in order to gain admission to this grotto of discovery that you have to be accompanied by a child). Eureka!'s pièce de resistance is the Global Garden; an environmental wonderland divided into seven different gardens based on different climates and narrated by the lovely Alan Titchmarsh.

Discovery Road, Halifax • 01422 330 012 • Open Daily 10am-5pm, Ages 3-12 • Adults £5.95, Children £5.95

### Flamingo Land

Theme park, zoo and holiday resort. Set in 375 acres it is one of the largest theme parks in the UK with more than 100 white-knuckle rides and slides, shows and also Europe's largest zoo, housing exotic animals including camels, lions, tigers, and polar bears. Rides include The Terroriser, Bullet, Wild Mouse, Top Gun, and Corkscrew.

Kirby Misperton, Malton, North Yorkshire • 01653 668 287 • Open Mon-Fri 10am-5pm, Sun-Sun and Bank Holidays 10am-6pm • Adults £14.50, Children £14.50, OAP £7.25, Family ticket £54

### Forbidden Corner

A curious blend of follies, mazes and puzzles: wander round the garden solving clues as you go, but watch out for the hidden water jets!

Tupgill Park Estate, Coverham, Middleham, Leyburn, North Yorkshire • 01969 640 638 • Open 12-6pm • Adults £6, Children £4, OAP £5

### Horsforth Village Museum

Horsforth, once described as the largest village in England, has somehow managed to retain some of its village identity and character in spite of being absorbed into the urban sprawl of Leeds. The museum aims to reflect this heritage through exhibitions drawn from all aspects of life in and around Horsforth village. Housed in the former council chambers it has an atmosphere and friendliness only to be found in a committed local history museum.

The Green, Horsforth, Leeds • 0113 268 3045 • Open Sat 10am-4pm, Sun 2-5pm • Free

### How Stean Gorge

Hidden limestone gorge in Nidderdale, North Yorkshire with 80ft deep ravine, lush vegetation and

Eureka!

# Museums & Places to Visit

Magna

sounds of the recreated dwellings to the dressed up tour guides and spectacular costumery. Go prepared to queue for a long time.
*Coppergate, York • 01904 543 402 • Open 31 Mar-2 Nov: daily 10am-5pm, 3 Nov-31 Mar 2004: daily 10am-4pm, Visit time 1 hour • Adults £7.20, Children £5.10, Students £6.10, OAP £6.10, Family ticket £21.95-£26.50*

### Keighley Bus Museum
A large collection of public transport buses, including 25 in running order and over 35 undergoing restoration. The museum also owns nine running vehicles, dating from 1927 to 1968 from the closed 'Transperience' museum in Bradford.
*Old Dalton Lane Depot, Old Dalton Lane, Keighley • 01282 413179 • Open 01282 413179 for details*

### Leeds Museum Resource Centre
Contains such delights as an Egyptian Mummy, Bengal tigers and Irish Elk. Guided tours available as well as activity workshops on Ancient Egypt, Greece and Rome, Fossils, Wildlife and Skeletons.
*Moorfield Road, Moorfield Industrial Estate, Yeadon, Leeds • 0113 214 6526 • Open 10am-4pm, booking essential • Adults £, Students £, Children £, OAP • Free*

### Lightwater Valley
A whole park completely devoted to rides of all shapes and sizes for all ages and sizes. Sound like heaven? Lightwater Valley in Ripon is just that when you have a big family with different tastes to cater for. The park is divided into 'Jaw Droppers' (for big people), Whipper Snappers (for medium people) and Nippers (for little'uns) and each ride comes with particular descriptions of what to expect should Auntie Vera fancy a turn on the Black Widow's Web. There's a slow train to carry the fainthearted round the grounds. Watch out for the 'Valligators', baby Al, Sally and Harry who prance round the park informing, amusing and generally badgering visitors.
*North Stainley, Ripon, North Yorkshire • 0870 458 0060 • Open 10am-4.30pm • Adults £13.50, Children £12*

### Magna
'Mum, are we there yet?'. If you fancy going a bit further afield, you could do worse than to make the trek to Rotherham to the marvellous Magna, 'the UK's first Science Adventure Centre', combining science, nature, history and fun (can they really go together in the same sentence, dad?), Magna has four adventure pavilions and an outdoor adventure park where in one day you can absorb the drama and excitement of the steel-making process in 'The Big Melt', debate the redevelopment of a coalmine and watch living robots in action. Perfect for more than one visit, Magna is

aquatic wildlife. 'Tom Taylor's Cave' is a small cave open to the public where children can try their hand at safe caving. There is also a licensed restaurant serving homemade food and a children's play area.
*Lofthouse, Pateley Bridge, North Yorkshire • 01423 755 666 • Open Daily 10am-6pm 01423 755 666*

### Ilkley Toy Museum
One of the best private toy collections in England, including dolls' houses, dolls, teddy bears and games. Exhibits date from as long ago as 350BC to the present day, with examples of play from practically every date in between. There is a shop selling replica antique games and toys as well as up-to-date gifts.
*Whitton Croft Road, Ilkley • 01943 603 855 • Open Sat-Sun and Bank Holidays 12-4pm. Winter and summer weekday times vary • Adults £3, Children £2, Family ticket £8*

### Ingleborough Cave
Spectacular limestone in the underground cave with impressive floodlit cave stalactites & stalagmites up to 350 million years old. There is a guided journey through the cave which has large passages and no steps, making it suitable for pushchairs and wheelchairs. There is also a shop selling souvenirs as well as hot and cold drinks.
*Clapham, North Yorkshire • 01524 251 242 • Open 31 Mar-31 Oct daily 10am-5pm. 1 Nov-30 Mar Sat-Sun 10am-5pm*

### Jorvik
Surely needs little explanation. A nationally renowned museum of Vikings, Norsemen and all things horned. This is a great day out (and you *need* a day) for all the family from the authentic smells (yes — all smells) and

Press and Feel...

**Please touch the exhibits.**

At Eureka! nothing is out of reach, with over 400 hands-on exhibits to touch, twist, pull and push – it's a bigger day out than you think!

Push and Pull...

Twist and Turn!

For more information call 07626 983191 or click on www.eureka.org.uk

the museum for children

Discovery Road, Halifax, West Yorkshire, HX1 2NE

NMPFT

## National Museum of Photography, Film and Television

A great journey through the history of all things media, from the Tudor 'camera obscura' through the very first wax cylinder to state of the art virtual reality systems. The museum operates over several floors, each one being dedicated to a different field of media, mostly reassuringly static but occasionally breaking into a whole new innovative display or demonstration. There really is (cliché cliché) something for all ages, from the fantastic magic carpet ride (where you can choose to fly over deserts or country houses) and the have-a-go film set, to the primitive zootropes and halls of mirrors. You can even sit Dad in TV Heaven watching Joanna Lumley in a tight leather catsuit, when he gets bored. There's a café as well as upstairs eating area, so you can let them loose on the cheese strings while you sup on the picnic of your choice.
*Pictureville, Bradford • 01274 202 030 • Open Daily 10am-5pm • Free*

family friendly, with an under-fives play area, packed lunch spot and the spectacular 'Red Hall Café'.
*Sheffield Road, Templeborough, Rotherham • 01709 720002 • Family ticket £26.00, Adults £8, Children £6*

## Mother Shiptons Caves

Cave and petrifying well where England's most famous prophetess lived during the reign of Henry VIII and Elizabeth I. There is also the Historia museum charting Knaresborough's history,
*Prosperity House, Highbridge, Knaresborough • 01423 864 600 • Open 1 Mar-31 Oct daily 9.30am-5.45pm. Nov/Feb Sat-Sun (except daily during Feb half-term) 10am-4.30pm*

## Museum of Rail Travel

Hands-on museum where you can sit in restored railway carriages and see how steam locomotives operate. There are video and audio demonstrations as well as a shop selling railway memorabilia.
*Ingrow Railway Centre, Keighley • 01535 680 425 • Open Daily, phone +44 (0)1535 680 425 for further details. • Adults £1, Children £1, OAP £1*

## National Coal Mining Museum

The museum gives children the opportunity to see what a miner's life is really like, with interactive exhibitions and displays, audio-visual plasma screens and retired pit ponies. There is also the chance to travel 140 metres underground with a helmet and lamp in a cage with a local miner as a guide.
*Caphouse Colliery, Overton, Wakefield • 01924 848 806 • Open 10am-5pm, last tour 3.30pm • Free*

## National Railway Museum

Largest railway museum in the world with large collection of railway memorabilia and photographic displays. There are rides on a miniature railway and full size trains as well as a designated children's play area.
*Leeman Road, York • 01904 621 261 • Open Daily 10am-6pm except 24-26 Dec • Free*

## Peace Museum

Complementing Bradford University's Department of Peace Studies, this museum has a blossoming archive of 'peace' memorabilia including films, books, paintings, photographs, posters and sculpture.
*10 Piece Hall Yard, Bradford • 01274 754 009 • Open Wed/Fri 11am-3pm, by appointment other times*

## Pontefract Museum

Pontefract's history from modern times to the present day displaying historical memorabilia from life under siege at Pontefract Castle during the civil war and life in the famous liquorice factories. There are also temporary touring exhibitions as well as in-house displays. The museum holds workshops for children and has a resource centre for educational groups.
*Slater Row, Pontefract • 01977 722740 • Open Mon-Sat:10am-4.30pm • Free*

## Prison & Police Museum

Museum tracing the history of law, order and punishment. Housed in the original Ripon prison, the exhibition spans the ground floor and nine prison cells, each one dedicated to different forms of punishment and prison conditions. Children will be able to see medieval stocks, pillories and whipping posts.

*St Marygate, Ripon, North Yorkshire • 01765 690799 • Open Apr and Oct: 1-4pm, May, Jun, Sep: 1-5pm, Jul-Aug 11am-5pm • Adults £2, Children £1.50*

### RHS Garden Harlow Carr

This extensive Royal Horticultural Society garden has a family trail and regularly puts on holiday activities for kids, including 'Fungus Event' and the more wholesome-sounding 'Apple Day'.

*Crag Lane, Harrogate • 01423 565418 • Open daily 9.30am-6pm • Adults £4.50, Students £2, Children £1, OAP £4*

### The Royal Armouries

Little boys with swords and helmets. Yadda yadda yadda. But no, it's not like that at ALL. The Royal Armouries Museum has one of the most exciting historical and informative collections in the country. Comprising five galleries chock full of memorabilia from the Dark Ages to 'modern times', it boasts world-renowned artefacts like Henry VIII's tournament armour and the only surviving elephant armour on display anywhere. Ever. As well as the regular weekend hands-on activities and static exhibitions, visitors can marvel at displays of jousting, falconry and different types of hand-to-hand combat. There is a licensed bistro and coffee shop serving hot and cold meals as well as a gift shop and library for public use.

*Armouries Drive, Leeds • 0113 220 1999 • Open Daily 10am-5pm, except 24 and 25 Dec • Free*

### Royal Pump Room Museum

Housed over the famous sulphur wells where for years people came to be 'cured', the museum houses a programme of changing exhibitions telling the story of Harrogate and allows you to sample the strongest sulphur water in Europe.

*Crown Place, Harrogate, North Yorkshire • 01423 556 188 • Open Mon-Sat 10am-5pm, Sun 2-5pm • Adults £2.50, OAP £1.50, Students £1.50, Children £1.25, Family ticket £5.50*

### Ryedale Folk Museum

Original domestic buildings from Ryedale villages, spread over a three-acre site and showing life in the area from medieval to present times. The museum holds regular open days on everything from farm machinery to historic cookery.

*Hutton le Hole, York • 01751 417 367 • Open Daily 10am-5.30pm • Adults £3.50, Children £2*

### Sewerby Hall Museum

Houses collections of regional arts and crafts as well as the East Yorkshire Photography Gallery and the Amy Johnson Room displaying the famous flyer's trophies and memorabilia. There are also extensive grounds set in over 50 acres of parkland with a children's zoo, containing monkeys, llamas and penguins along with an adventure playground for children of all ages and pitch and putt and bowls for the mums and dads.

*Church Lane, Sewerby, East Yorkshire • 01262 677 874 • Open 18th Apr-28 Sep 2003 daily 10am-5.30pm • Adults £3.10, Children £1.20*

Royal Armouries

### Stump Cross Caverns

Discovered in 1858 by miners looking for lead, Stump Cross Caverns are open to the public with guided tours, video shows, detailed discussions on current academic research to investigate stalagmite drip rates with computerised data.

*Greenhow, Pateley Bridge, North Yorkshire • 01756 752 780 • Open mid Mar-31 Oct daily 10am-4pm. 1 Nov-mid Mar Sat-Sun 10am-4pm • Free*

### Thackray Medical Museum

Galleries, collections and interactive displays charting the history of disease, grime and all things unsavoury. There are several galleries, collections and interactive displays where children can discover everything from common illnesses and antibiotics to major surgical practices. There is also a café and gift shop.

*131 Beckett Street, Leeds • 0113 244 4343 • Open Tue-Sun and Bank Holiday Mon 10am-5pm Adults £4.40, children £3.30*

### The Deep

Housed in one of the country's most intriguing buildings, the world's first 'submarium' is an exciting and state of the art journey beneath the surface of the waves into a fascinating and mind-boggling history. The Deep contains the world's only underwater lift (admittedly, not everyone's idea of fun ... ) and Europe's deepest tank. The centre contains seven species of shark, including Britain's only Grey Reef Shark.

*Hull • 01482 381 000 • Open daily 10am-6pm except 24-25 Dec • Adults £6.50, OAP £4.50, Children £4, Family ticket £19-£21*

### Thorpe Perrow Arboretum

An 85-acre collection of trees which is also home to a fearsome collection of hawks, falcons, eagles, owls and even vultures, with daily flying demonstrations and a chance to 'meet' the birds.

*Bedale, North Yorkshire • 01677 425 323 • Open daily dawn to dusk, with exceptions in winter • Adults £5.25, OAP £4, Children £2.75*

### Thwaite Mills

Water-powered putty grinding mill with two giant waterwheels built in 1825 and the only preserved putty grinding mill. The mill is set in 10-acre parkland on an island in the River Aire and also has the original Georgian mill manager's house and engineering workshop.

*Tropical World*

Thwaite Lane, Stourton, Leeds • 0113 249 6453 •
Open Mon-Thu and Sat 10am-5pm, Sun 1-5pm • Adults
£2, Children 50p, Students £1

### Tolson Museum
Museum of the history of Huddersfield and Kirklees
with exciting displays and exhibitions. Kids can discover
aspects of local history alongside instruction in
prehistory, evolution and the history of transport.
There is also 'Ronnie the Raven's Puzzlepath', an
under-fives' trail around the museum.
Ravensknowle Park, Huddersfield • 01484 223 830 •
Open Mon-Fri 11am-5pm, Sat-Sun 12pm-5pm • Free

### Tropical World
A heady mix of monkeys, butterflies, creepy crawlies
and exotic fish, the centre is situated very close to
Roundhay Park (if you need a quick game of frisbee
afterwards) and has recently been refurbished to
house even more curiosities. There is a small gift shop
as well as Coronation House, a stunning glasshouse
containing some very rare orchids.
1 Park Cottages, Prince's Avenue, Leeds • 0113 266
1850 • Open daily 10am-dusk • Adults £2, Children £1

### Wakefield Museum
Dedicated largely to the work and times of Wakefield's
famous son, explorer and pioneer of the world's first
nature reserve, Charles Waterton, the museum
contains memorabilia from his travels and a collection
of the rare species that he brought to the area and
preserved. There are also interactive displays and
digitalised photography apparatus.
Wood Street, Wakefield • 01924 305351 • Open Mon-
Sat 10.30am-4.30pm, Sun 2-4.30pm. • Free

### White Scar Cave
The longest show cave in Britain, covering one mile
and including the largest caverns in the country. See the
famous 200,000 year old Battlefield Cavern, over 330
feet long and walk past waterfalls, stalactites and
stalagmites.
Ingleton, North Yorkshire • 01524 241 244 • Open
10am-5.30pm • Adults £6.50, Children £3.50

### Workhouse Museum of Poor Law
Museum displaying the history of Yorkshire's poor,
from workhouses to the street, with restored vagrants'
wards and Victorian Hard Times Gallery.
Allhallowgate, Ripon, North Yorkshire • 01765 603006
• Open Good Fri-27 Oct daily 1-4pm, except 1 Jul-31
Aug 11am-4pm • Adults £2, Children 50p, Students
£1.50, OAP £1.50

### York Castle Museum
Museum housed in former prisons charting the last
400 years of York's history. The museum houses

The Royal Armouries Museum in Leeds was
officially opened by the Queen in July 1996 and is
home to a world-renowned collection of arms and
armour. Since Henry VIII's time the collection had
been housed at the Tower of London but lack of
space meant that only a very small part of the
collection was able to be displayed. The new Leeds
museum was purpose-built so that much more of
the collection could be put on show.

Five themed galleries: War, Tournament,
Oriental, Self Defence and Hunting display in excess
of 8000 permanent exhibits. Amongst the many
treasures are Henry VIII's tournament armour, the
awesome 16th-century Mogul elephant armour and
the beautifully intricate lion armour. The breath-
taking Hall of Steel — a 40m-high glass tower —
houses a huge display of over 3000 objects. Film
footage, video, interactives and handling collections
help to make learning enjoyable and stimulating for
everyone.

The Royal Armouries pride themselves on bringing
history to life by telling the stories of people whose
lives were touched by the objects on display. There
are performances throughout the day, by our team
of interpreters, who wear authentic costumes.
From April to October authentically re-created
jousting* takes place in the Tiltyard. Daily falconry
displays and the opportunity to see the birds and
horses up close in the Menagerie Court is an added
bonus.

*subject to events programme and weather
permitting

*York Minster*

stunning displays of costumery and playthings as well as reconstructed cobbles streets. Children can also experience the harshness of prison life in days gone by and see the cells in which the infamous Dick Turpin was locked.
*Castle Area, Eye of York, York • 01904 553 125 • Open Daily 9.30am-5pm • Adults £6, Student £3.50, OAP £3.50, Children £3.50, Family ticket £16*

### York Dungeon

York is one of the most haunted cities in Britain, allegedly playing host to over 150 ghosts. In the York Dungeon you have the opportunity to meet them all and relive their — often gory — stories, including that of the infamous Dick Turpin who was tried at York in the 1700s
*12 Clifford Street, York • 01904 632 599 • Open 10am-6.30pm except 25 Dec*

### York Minster

Visit the beautiful cathedral with its glorious gothic architecture and see the stunning restoration work on the roof bosses after the devastating 1980's fire as well as the beautiful 'rose window'. There is a café and gift shop.
*York • 1904 557 200 • Open 7am-4.30pm • Children £1, Adults £3.50, OAP £2.50*

### Yorkshire Air Museum

Museum based on a World War Two Bomber Command Station. Displays include the original Control Tower, Air Gunners' Collection, Barnes Wallis' prototype 'bouncing bomb' and an Airborne Forces Display. The collection of historical aircraft depicts aviation from its earliest days, to World War Two with the Halifax rebuild through to post war jets.
*Halifax Way, Elvington, York • 01904 608 595 • Open 30 Mar-25 Oct 2003: daily 10am - 5pm • Adults £5, Children £3, OAP £4*

### Yorkshire Museum & Gardens

Archaeological museum housing artefacts from Roman, Viking and Medieval times. There is a changing exhibitions programme in addition to the permanent displays of sculpture, mosaics and everyday items. Visitors also get the chance to see the famous Middleham jewel, a pendant of gold and sapphire once belonging to Richard III.
*Museum Gardens, York • 01904 551 800 • Open Daily 10am-5pm • Adults £4, Children £2.50, Students £2.50, OAP £2.50, Family ticket £10*

## Galleries

### Bankfield Museum

Regular textile-related workshops and demonstrations.
*Boothtown Road, Halifax • 01422 354 823 • Open Wed-Sun 12pm-5pm • Free*

### Cartwright Hall

Municipal gallery with such kids-friendly shows as the Lego exhibition and Back to the Future, involved in the Big Draw and In the Picture and regular venue for workshops and activities.
*Lister Park, Bradford • 01274 751 212 • Open Tue-Sat and Bank Holiday Mon 10am-5pm, Sun 1-5pm • Free*

### Hebden Bridge Sculpture Trail

Culture vultures can take an art-spotting stroll along five miles of woodland and river paths at National Trust-owned beauty spot Hardcastle Crags. Here they will find the work of local, national and international artists alongside work by local schools, colleges and community groups. This transitory show makes discovering the outdoor works great fun. For 2003's Trail Tom Barnett has produced a clay reproduction of Gibson Mill for which the little ones can make figures. Alongside this is Kevin Jacques' rain stick to summon the clouds to open, though given the Calderdale Valley's penchant for summer storms we may not really have to rely on its magical prowess.
*Sunnyview Cottage, Edge Lane, Colden, Hebden Bridge • 01422 842022 • Daily until 29 Jul 03 and then Jul 2004 • Free*

### Huddersfield Art Gallery

Municipal gallery with arts and crafts activities and a lively programme of cutting edge contemporary art that may, surprisingly, appeal to a younger audience.
*Princess Alexandra Walk, Huddersfield • 01484 221 964 • Open Mon-Fri 10am-5pm, Sat-Sun 12-5pm • Free*

### Leeds City Art Gallery

Themed workshops and activities to accompany the excellent range of exhibitions at this municipal gallery.
*The Headrow, Leeds • 0113 247 8248 • Open Mon-Fri 10am-5pm, Wed 10am-8pm, Sun 1-5pm, closed Bank Holidays • Free*

### National Museum of Photography, Film and Television

Resources and activities for the budding young photographer.
*Pictureville, Bradford • 01274 202 030 • Open Daily 10am-5pm • Free*

### Newby Hall

Richard and Lucinda Compton, owners of Newby Hall, prove that they have just as exquisite a taste for fine art as they have for horticulture in the gardens and design in the house itself. Much of the work is site specific and will appeal to kids with a love of natural forms (from fir cones to mushrooms) and the animal kingdom (from rams to tigers). Even the more abstract work is so sensitively placed in the gorgeous grounds of this splendid stately home that this makes an exciting and refreshing day out for all the family.
*Ripon • 01423 322583 • Open Tue-Sun 12-5pm • Adults £7.20, Children £4.70, OAP £6.20*

### Piece Hall

On alternate Saturdays there is a Saturday Art Club with art and craft activities for 8 to 12 year olds at the Arts Resource Centre and a the Gallery has a quiz and interactive Art Station with art materials available.
*Westgate, Halifax • 01422 358 087 • Open Tues-Sun 10am-5pm • Free*

### Wakefield Art Gallery

Run regular workshops and activities and 'Getting into Art' for under-5s
*Wentworth Terrace, Wakefield • 01924 305 796 • Open Tues-Sat 10.30am-4.30pm, Sun 2-4.30pm • Free*

### Yorkshire Sculpture Park

With a lively range of kids activities the YSP is a great place to combine a picnic with an introduction to the world of sculpture. There are some 244 square acres of landscaped grounds with a fabulous nature trail devised by Don Rankin. The Barbara Hepworth work may at first appear austere and cold but in situ they are vibrant and quite magical. Kids are well catered for too in the Visitor's Centre and there is a designated area where, on workshop days, you and family can have a go at creating a modern masterpiece yourselves!
*Bretton Hall, West Bretton, Wakefield • 01924 830 302 • Open Daily Grounds: 10am-6pm, Galleries: 11am-5pm • Free*

*Hebden Bridge Sculpture Trail*

Harewood House

## Houses and Castles

### Beningbrough Hall and Gardens
This Georgian mansion contains over 100 paintings, as well as a fully-equipped Victorian laundry and a walled garden.
*Beningbrough, York • 01904 470666 • Open House: Apr-Jun, Sep: Sat-Wed, Jul-Aug: Sun-Wed, Fri-Sat House: 12-5pm Grounds: 11am-5:30pm • Adults £4-£5.50, Children £2-£2.70, Family ticket £10-£13.50*

### Bolton Castle
A sternly imposing 14th-century stronghold, Bolton doesn't just look the part: its five floors contain tableaux depicting medieval life whilst events include re-enactments and dressing-up sessions for kids.
*Leyburn, North Yorkshire • 01969 623 981 • Open Apr-Sep 10am-5pm • Adults £4, Students £3, Children £3, OAP £3*

### Castle Howard
No medieval privies or vats of boiling oil to be found here: this 18th-century castle is a grandiose monument to the wealth and (often questionable) taste of the aristocracy. Kids may be less interested in the paintings by Gainsborough and Reynolds than in the three acres of rose gardens.
*York • 01653 648 333 • Open 14 Feb-2 Nov 2003 daily 10am-4.30pm • Adults £9, OAP £8, Students £8, Children £6*

### Cliffords Tower
The last remaining part of York's old castle sits impressively on a mound near the museum. Make it up the steps and you'll find displays explaining the tower's frequently gruesome history.
*Tower Street, York • 01904 646 940 • Open 1 Apr-30 Sep: daily 10am-6pm, Aug: 9.30am-7pm • Adults £2, Family ticket £5*

### East Riddlesden Hall
Romantically-crumbling 17th-century manor house with period furnishings and a colourful garden. Costumed tours throughout the summer add to the atmosphere.
*Bradford Road, Riddlesden, Keighley • 01535 607 075 • Open 29 Mar-29 Jun and 1 Sep-2 Nov Tue-Wed and Sat-Sun 12-5pm. 1 Jul-31 Aug Mon-Wed and Sat-Sun 12-5pm • Children £1.80, Adults £3.60, Family ticket £9*

### Fort Paull
Yorkshire's only surviving Napoleonic fort. The site itself was used as a Viking watch point and the displays reflect the diverse cast of characters to have passed through the region. There is a junior assault course with a rope swing and tunnels as well as rifle range and archery field and licensed restaurant and tearooms.
*Battery Road, Paull, Hull • 01482 882 655 • Open daily 10am-6pm, may change in winter • Adults £4, Children £3, Family ticket £12*

### Harewood House
This famed stately home contains a wealth of luxurious furnishings, paintings and knick-knacks whilst the art gallery regularly hosts cutting-edge exhibitions. However it's more likely that kids will be entranced by the colourful residents of the bird garden or enjoy exploring the Capability Brown-sculpted gardens or clambering over the adventure playground.
*Harewood, Leeds • 0113 218 1010 • Adults £9.50, Children £5.25, OAP £8.75*

### Knaresborough Castle
Partly demolished after the Civil War, enough remains of Knaresborough Castle for its dramatic and bloody history to be brought vividly to life by the guided tours. Shiver in the dank dungeons, scramble down the sallyport (escape tunnel) or just soak up some of the appealing views.

# Order your copy of Dining Out 03/04 now!

**OUT NOW**

Did you miss the Dining Out issue of The Leeds Guide? If so, you also missed out on your free copy of Dining Out 03/04: the essential full-colour guide to dining in Leeds, Bradford and Harrogate, packed with profiles, listings and information about places to eat and drink. But you can still get hold of your own copy, as Dining Out is now available to buy in shops around the region. Or you can have it delivered direct to your door by filling out the order form below.

## Dining Out 03/04
BRADFORD HARROGATE LEEDS

I would like to order ...... copies of Dining Out 03/04 at £2.95 each

Add 75p per copy for postage and packing

Total £ . . . . . . . . . . . . . . . . . . . . .

I enclose a cheque/postal order made payable to Leeds Guide Ltd

☐

Please charge my credit/debit card

(Delta, Mastercard, Visa, Visa Electron, JCB

☐  Cards, Solo, Switch)

Card No (long no. in middle of card):

| | | | | | | | | | | | | | | | | | | |

Start Date: | | | |

Expiry Date: | | | |

Issue No (Switch): | |

Name: . . . . . . . . . . . . . . . . . . . . . . . . . . . . . . . . . . . . . . . . . . . . . . . . . . .

Address:. . . . . . . . . . . . . . . . . . . . . . . . . . . . . . . . . . . . . . . . . . . . . . . . . . .

. . . . . . . . . . . . . . . . . . . . . . . . . . . . . . . . . . . . . . . . . . . . . . . . . . . . . . . . . .

Daytime/mobile tel:. . . . . . . . . . . . . . . . . . . . . . . . . . . . . . . . . . . . . . . . . . .

Date:. . . . . . . . . . . . . . . . . . . . Signed:. . . . . . . . . . . . . . . . . . . . . . . . . . . . .

Return form to: The Leeds Guide, Freepost NEA 3320, Leeds, LS1 1YY

Please tick here ☐ if you do not wish to hear of further Leeds Guide offers or events.

*Castle Yard, Knaresborough • 01423 556 188 • Open Good Fri-end Sep daily 10.30am-5pm • Adults £2, OAP £1.50, Children £1.25, Family ticket £5.50*

## Lotherton Hall

This council-owned house and art gallery has a large deer park and a bird garden containing eagles, kookaburras and a pair of Andean Condors.

*Lotherton Lane, Aberford, Leeds • 0113 281 3259 • Open Mar-Dec Tue-Sat 10am-5pm, 10am-4pm in winter, Sun 1-5pm, 12-4pm in winter • Adults £2, OAP £1, Students £1, Children 50p*

## Nostell Priory

Amongst the Chippendale furniture and paintings by Brueghel the Younger is an 18th-century dolls' house with its original fittings. There's also a rose garden and kids' play area.

*Mansion House, Nostell Priory Estate, Nostell, Wakefield • 01924 863 892 • Open end March to end October Wed-Sun and Bank Holiday Mon 1-5.30pm. Nov Sat-Sun 1-5.30pm • Adults £5, Children £2, Family ticket £12.50*

## Nunnington Hall

A nursery, 'haunted' rooms and an attic full of miniature rooms will all be of interest to the smaller visitor in this 17th-century house.

*Nunnington, York • 01439 748 283 • Open 22 Mar-30 Apr and 1 Oct-2 Nov Wed-Sun 1:30-4:30pm. 1-31 May and 1-30 Sep Wed-Sun 1.30-5pm. 1 Jun-31 Aug Tue-Sun 1:30-5pm • Adults £4.50, Children £2, Family ticket £11*

## Ripley Castle

Ripley Castle can be seen through a guided tour, which visitors in on the many exploits of the Ingilbys, residents since 1320. Capability Brown-landscaped gardens offer plenty of opportunity for leg-stretching.

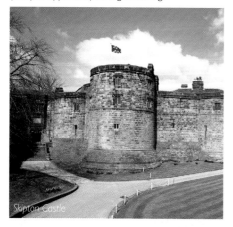

Skipton Castle

*Ripley, Harrogate • Open Jan-May and Sep-Dec Tue-Thu and Sat-Sun 10.30am-3pm. Jun-Aug daily 10.30am-3pm • Adults £6, OAP £5, Children £3.50*

## Sandal Castle

Remember the mnemonic "Richard Of York Gave Battle In Vain"? Well, this is where he did it. Nowdays the castle is mainly earthworks and a few stony bits, but a couple of plastic swords and some imagination should suffice for an afternoon's battle re-enactment.

*Manygates Lane, Wakefield • 01924 249 779 • Open daily • Free*

## Scarborough Castle

Overlooking the resort's two bays, this castle has been battered many times between Norman times and the present. The lively audio guides (included in the admission fee) help bring the keep, curtain walls and various ruins to life, with impressive sea views to boot.

*Castle Road, Scarborough • 01723 372 451 • Open 1 Apr-30 Sep daily 10am-6pm. 1-31 Oct daily 10am-5pm. 1 Nov-31 Mar daily 10am-4pm except 24-26 Dec and 1 Jan • Adults £3, Children £1.50, Family ticket £7.50*

## Shibden Hall

A stately home in the heart of the beautiful Halifax countryside, with permanent displays of old farm machinery as well as frequent craft fairs and exhibitions. There are a group of old workshops demonstrating different trades together with different grades of workers' housing and an old bar where the Luddites plotted.

*Lister's Road, Halifax • 01422 352246 • Open Mar-Nov: Mon-Sat 10am-5pm, last admission 4.15pm, Sunday 12-5pm. • Adults £3.50, Children £2.50*

## Skipton Castle

Over 900 years old, this well-preserved fort overlooks the canal and was a Royalist stronghold during the Civil War: its central court is still dominated by a marvellously twisty yew that was planted in 1659. An informative factsheet helps bring the rooms to life.

*Skipton, North Yorkshire • 01756 792 442 • Open Daily from 10am • Adults £4.80, Children £2.40, OAP £4.20, Students £4.20*

## Treasurers House

This treasure trove of artefacts from the 16th and 20th centuries offers both a guide and a quiz trail so that families can discover the contents together.

*Minster House, York • 01904 624 247 • 22 Mar-28 Sep Mon-Thu and Sat-Sun 11am-4.30pm • Adults £4, Children £2, Family ticket £10*

Parks, Farms & Railways

*Embsay & Bolton Abbey Steam Railway*

## Parks

Cities such as Leeds and Bradford were notorious in Victorian times for their dirt, smoke and over-crowding. This led to the creation of some of today's best-loved parks, which have gradually developed the individual characters that each have today. At the same time it has become much easier to reach the surrounding countryside and you don't have to go far to find places where kids can run off some excess energy while you sit back and enjoy the views.

### Bolton Abbey

Not an abbey (although there is a ruined priory onsite) but a large park belonging to the Duke and Duchess of Devonshire, Bolton Abbey is incredibly popular in summer, acting as a kind of beach substitute for the people of Bradford district. The banks of the river running through the valley soon become lined with families picnicking and bathing: if you're looking for a more peaceful side, fields and wooded paths stretch far enough for a good wander.
*Skipton, North Yorkshire*

### Brimham Rocks

These curious-shaped rock formations are part of a National Trust park and are popular with families wanting to spot the 'Dancing Bear' or 'The Watchdog' whilst having a picnic. Extra fun can be had by scaring your kids with the threat of pushing the (apparently) precariously-balanced rocks over on them.
*Summerbridge, Harrogate*

### Golden Acre Park

The site of 1930s 'pleasure gardens' that soon went out of business, the spacious Golden Acre Park has everything you'd expect in a traditional park: a bandstand — with brass band concerts at weekends — flowerbeds, a lake with ducks and a café selling ice-creams and snacks. The downside is that its location on the outer stretches of Otley Road (with a pretty infrequent bus service on Sundays) requires special effort to visit. Once you get there, though, the woody wildlife reserve on the other side of the road is also worth a look for nature-loving kids.
*Otley Road, Bramhope, Leeds*

### Hyde Park

The nearest park of any size to Leeds City Centre, Hyde Park — or Woodhouse Moor to give it its official name — is mainly short grass with a few lines of trees, making it good for games of football or running around. It has a skate ramp and basketball courts, making it popular with both local families and students: the two sides of the family come together each summer for Unity Day, a free festival of music and entertainment that shows true community spirit.
*Woodhouse Lane, Leeds*

### Lister Park, Bradford

The grounds of what is now Cartwright Hall Art Gallery, Lister Park has undergone restoration in the past few years: as well as a spruced-up boating lake and botanical gardens, there's a café, adventure playground and a new feature, the Mughal Water Gardens. Inspired by the styles of gardens from hundreds of

Hyde Park

years ago in what is now northern India and Pakistan, the gardens are based on rectangular designs, combining grassed areas, paths and avenues of trees with small streams, waterfalls, fountains and ponds. The history will probably come second to the joy of splashing people, though.
*Bradford*

### Lotherton Hall Gardens
Part of a council-owned stately home on the outskirts of Leeds, Lotherton Hall Gardens are notable the herd of deer which can be watched from the edge of their enclosure. As well as formal gardens, there are hazel and ash coppices to explore, with trails to follow.
*Lotherton Lane, Aberford, Leeds*

### Middleton Park
A massive 600 acres — 200 of which are protected woodland — Middleton Park is ideal for strolls among the ancient oaks and streams, spotting flowers, fungi and creatures as you go. It's also a destination for the Middleton Railway — see the Railways section for details.
*Middleton Park Avenue, Leeds*

### Otley Chevin
Every Boxing Day, a group of running enthusiasts (some would have less complimentary names for them) work off the previous day's dinner by running to the top of this steep hill. We wouldn't recommend this, but once you've struggled to the top (the steps help, and there are less steep, less direct routes), kids can have fun spotting landmarks such as nearby reservoirs and the planes taking off from Leeds-Bradford airport.
*Otley*

### Peel Park
Bradford's largest park plays host to its annual Mela, a fun family day out of music, food and entertainment. The natural valley sweeps down to a lake and it's also near to the Leeds-Bradford Canal.
*Bradford*

### Potternewton Park
As well as providing a rare patch of green in one of the city's most densely-built areas, Potternewton Park plays host to the Chapeltown Carnival every August Bank Holiday weekend.
*Chapeltown, Leeds*

### Roundhay Park and Canal Gardens
Now then, now then; you may just spot Sir Jimmy Saville jogging his way around this giant North Leeds expanse which his flat overlooks. But the kids are more likely to be absorbed by feeding the ducks and geese on the lake or playing 'King of the Castle' around the

Meanwood Valley Urban Farm

turreted folly. There's a café to replenish your energy, whilst across the road the lies the more formal Canal Gardens and Tropical World, which is always worth a visit.
*Roundhay road, Leeds. See Museums section for Tropical World*

### The Stray
Nothing out of the ordinary, The Stray is nevertheless conveniently located right in the centre of Harrogate. Its green stretches and tree-lined avenues seem to go on forever — good for wobbly learner cyclists who want to shed those stabilisers.
*Harrogate*

### Temple Newsam Park
Home until this year of the Leeds Festival, the large open spaces of the Temple Newsam estate also play host to Party in the Park and Opera in the Park. Despite this, it's surprisingly hard to reach by bus, with the only direct services on Sundays: the rest of the time it's a 10-15 minute walk from the bus stop. However, the visitor farm and newly-reopened house add to its attractions, whilst near the house you'll find a herb garden and a rhododendron walk.
*Temple Newsam Road, Temple Newsam, Leeds*

### Yeadon Tarn
There's a playground here, but the main selling point is the large lake that's home to a yachting club. Cue free entertainment watching colourful sails and the occasional capsize. Add in the proximity to Leeds-Bradford Airport and you've got more transport action than a Fisher-Price set.
*Yeadon, Leeds*

## Visitor Farms

**Farms can be mysterious and dangerous places and these child-friendly ones are a safe way for kids to learn about animals and the countryside. At the same time they provide good examples of how non-intensive and organic methods can work and help conserve many of the rare breeds which have all but disappeared today.**

### Bradford City Farm
A working farm were kids can encounter animals and learn about their care. As well as horticultural and environmental education, the farm also offers a woodland walk and a wildlife pond.
*Walker Drive, Girlington, Bradford • 01274 543 500 • Open 1 Oct-Easter: Tue-Thu/Sun 9.30am-4pm. Easter-30 Sep: Tue-Thu/Sun 9.30am-4.30pm • Adults Free*

### Hazel Brow Farm
This 200-acre organic farm allows kids to observe and take part in some of its everyday activities, from chatting to the farmer whilst the cows are being milked to bottle-feeding lambs — they can even watch them being born, if you don't mind fielding a few awkward questions on the way home. As well as a café and giftshop, the farm lays on craft demonstrations and produces free guide-packs to walks in the area.
*Low Row, Richmond, North Yorkshire • 01748 886 224 • Open 30 Mar-30 Sep Tue-Thu, Sat-Sun and Bank Holiday Mon 11am-6pm • Adults £4, Children £3.50, Family ticket £14.00*

### Home Farm
Part of the Temple Newsam Estate, Home Farm is the largest Rare Breeds centre in the country, with over 400 animals including pigs, goats and poultry. The Georgian and Victorian farm buildings also host demonstrations of traditional countryside crafts such as blacksmithing and butter-making.
*Temple Newsam Estate, Leeds • 0113 264 5535 • Open Until 25 Oct Tue-Sun and Bank Holiday Mon 10am-5pm. 26 Oct-27 Mar 2004 Tue-Sun 10am-4pm. 28 Mar-31 Oct 2004 Tue-Sun and Bank Holiday Mon 10am-5pm • Adults £3, Children £2*

### Meanwood Valley Urban Farm
As well as helping to conserve rare breeds and local wildlife, this 14-acre oasis in North Leeds provides a vital opportunity for city kids to experience the countryside and learn about the environment. Pigs, sheep, goats and poultry nestle alongside community allotments, a bird-feeding station and a shop selling the farm's organic produce. Wide paths make the farm an unusually wheelchair- and pushchair-friendly one.
*Sugar Mill Road, Leeds • 0113 262 9759 • Open Tue-Sun 10am-4pm • Adults £1, Children 50p*

### Monk Park Farm
Wallabies, fallow deer and llamas are some of the more unusual species to be found at this farm, along with rare breeds of sheep, dinky Shetland ponies and imposing Highland cattle. As well as feeding the animals and falling in love with the tame lambs, kids get an adventure playground and can watch sheepdog trialling on Sundays.

Bagby, Thirsk, North Yorkshire • 01845 597730 • *Open Mar Sat-Sun 11am-5.30pm, 1 Apr-26 Oct daily 11am-5.30pm • Adults £3.50, Children £2.50, OAP £2.50*

## Railways

The railway closures of the 1960s only seemed to give new drive to leagues of railway enthusiasts who have lovingly restored many of the lines or replaced them with narrow-gauge track. Many of these railways pass through some of Yorkshire's most stunning countryside: kids will love the drama of the puffing steam engines and the curiously old-fashioned stations. They tend to all run on time, too.

### Abbey Light Railway

Narrow-gauge railway built by enthusiasts running a short but picturesque journey around the grounds of Kirkstall Abbey (ideal for a picnic afterwards!) with diesel and electric locomotives and open-sided carriages.
*Bridge Road, Kirkstall, Leeds • 0113 267 5087 • Open Sun and Bank Holiday Mon*

### Embsay & Bolton Abbey Steam Railway

This railway takes in the delights of the edges of the Yorkshire Dales, stopping at the ideal picnic destination of Bolton Abbey. However, with a variety of trains ranging from 1960s diesel, steam trains, luxury 'Stately

Trains' and the odd appearance from Thomas the Tank Engine, kids may well be too busy looking anywhere *but* out of the window to notice.
*Bolton Abbey Station, Bolton Abbey, Skipton, North Yorkshire • 01756 710 614 • Open 15 Jul-31 Aug daily, 10.30am-5.10pm. Jan-Mar Sun 10.30am-5.10pm. Apr-Jun & Sep-Dec Sat-Sun and selected weekdays 10.30am-5.10pm. • Adults £6, Children £3, Family ticket £16.00*

### Keighley & Worth Valley Railway

Running from Keighley to Oxenhope, this restored line passes through Oakworth station, where adults can relive their memories of *The Railway Children*. Although this nostalgia will be lost on most people under 35, the railway — which regularly runs steam engines — still has many attractions, including tunnels, embankments and Britain's smallest station at Damems.
*The Railway Station, Haworth, Keighley • 01535 642 323 • Open All year: Sat-Sun 9.15am-6pm (4.30pm in winter), plus summer weekdays 10.10am-4.55pm • Adults £7-£10, Children £3.50-£5, Family ticket £19.00-£25.00*

### Kirklees Light Railway

Offering an eight-mile return journey along the route of the former Lancashire & Yorkshire Clayton West Branch Line with some lovely countryside on the way, this narrow-gauge railway uses steam locomotives

*Embsay & Bolton Abbey Steam Railway*

Shipley Glen Tramway

with both open and covered carriages (which also have heating). As well as the trains themselves, the railway also offers a mini-ride around the duck pond, displays of model steam trains, kid-size fairground rides, a gift shop and picnic areas.

*Railway Station, Park Mill Way, Clayton West, Huddersfield • 01484 865727 • Open 26 May-1 Sep*

*daily, 2 Sep-25 May Sat-Sun. Trains hourly from 11am • Adults £5.50, Children £3.50, Family ticket £16.00*

### Middleton Railway

Established in 1758, the Middleton railway is the world's oldest and was the first to earn revenue from steam trains. It runs approximately one mile between Hunslet and Middleton, staffed, like many such railways, by enthusiastic volunteers.

*The Station, Moor Road, Leeds • 0113 271 0320 • Adults £2.50, Children £1.50, Family ticket £7*

### Shipley Glen Tramway

Baildon moor above Saltaire was where Bradford's Victorian millworkers came to breathe fresh air and enjoy the delights of the funfair, the Japanese gardens and the Temperance Tearoom. Nowdays a small fairground is all that remains; but the journey up to the moor is fun in its own right when made with the help of this funicular tramway, with its two open-sided trains which alternately rattle their way up and down through the wooded glen.

*Prod Lane, Baildon, Shipley • 01274 589 010 • Open Jan-Feb/Nov: Sun 12-4pm. Mar/Dec: Sat 1-4pm, Sun 12-4pm. Apr-Oct: Sat 12-5pm, Sun 11am-6pm, plus May-Aug: Bank Holiday Mon 10am-6pm. • Adults 60p, Children 40p*

Embsay & Bolton Abbey Steam Railway

Shopping

*Early Learning Centre*

## Toyshops

**Looking for this year's Christmas craze, or for something more unusual? Try these ...**

### Early Learning Centre

Everyone knows children learn through play. And the Early Learning Centre champions this. So if you want yours to grow up to be the new Einstein, come and talk to one of the assistants here. Not only do they enjoy helping people choose the right toy, they also have great product knowledge. And younger children aren't excluded. They stock items such as flash cards to ensure that even the youngest child can have a head start at the Nobel prize for literature. And just because it's good for them, doesn't mean the Early Learning Centre's not fun. They leave toys out so children can play to their heart's content while you discuss their glowing future.

*17 Bond Street Centre, Bond Street, Leeds • 0113 243 4799*

### Formative Fun

In a similar vein to the Early learning Centre, Formative Fun stocks toys that are fun and educational. In fact, some of them look downright intriguing. Fancy starting an ant farm, growing crystals or caring for some Sea Monkeys? Then this is the place to visit. You won't be stuck if you're looking for help either. There's an army of assistants to choose from.

*9 Beulah Street, Harrogate • 01423 501 157*

### Rocking Horse

Traditional toys at Sensible Prices, it says on the door. And they're not kidding! It's heart-warming to see that there are some people that still believe a toy doesn't have to have batteries to be fun. You'll find some real classics here. Model boats, a wooden fort, train sets, and yes — rocking horses. They also stock doll's houses and an amazing selection of furniture. Toys like they used to be.

*2c Cheltenham Parade, Harrogate • 01423 566718*

### The Toy Shop

Giant inflatable banana anyone? When you see the diverse range of toys on this stall, you'll quickly realise it's filled with 'whatever I can get my hands on' rather than carefully chosen from a stock catalogue, unless of course, the owner has amazingly eclectic taste. And that's a good thing. This isn't the kind of place you come when you have a specific item in mind; it's a fun place to spend a couple of pounds. Hula hoop? Dumper truck? Airfix kit anyone?

*Kirkgate Market, Leeds • 0113 246 0387*

### Tierneys Traditional Toys

One of those places the grown-ups enjoy as much, if not more, than the children. Making high quality dolls' houses and furniture on site, they've an impressive selection in their huge showroom. They also stock a whole range of traditional toys, including kites,

*Early Learning Centre*

puppets, castles, farms, rocking houses and even toy boxes.
*Wesley Place, Wellington Road, Dewsbury • 01924 463 968*

### Toy Box
Set away from the main shopping area, this small shop reminds you of the ones that you used to see on every high street. Expect a cheerful welcome and as much or little help as you need while you browse the shelves. Corgi model cars, wooden spinning tops and pocket money toys — it'll take you back a bit!
*184 Kings Road, Harrogate • 01423 701 709*

### Toymaster
Now this is a great idea. Take locally owned specialist toy shops, bring them all together, and what have you got? The perfect combination of friendly service and buying power. This means you can expect to be helped by someone who really knows about toys and can bring their own personality to the shop. And you don't have to pay through the nose for it. Brilliant.
*47-49 James Street, Harrogate • 01423 564 335*

### Toys R Us
This is one of those places where you feel like you need to be wearing walking shoes. It's a huge warehouse of a place, stocking quite literally everything. Well, unless you're looking for this year's must-have item which will be sold out. But that's not Toys 'R' Us, that's life. So they try really hard, even letting you pre-order some sought after items. There's also a good selection of consoles and games for older kids. A word of advice — be careful if you're looking for Barbie things. Virtually an entire aisle is devoted to her and her accessories. And with all that pink, it's enough to make your eyes bleed.
*Gelderd Road, Birstall, Batley, West Yorkshire • 01924 420 556*

### Toyworld
Discount villages, discount centres — they're everywhere. And if you get a kick out of buying famous branded goods at a fraction of the price in the stores, you'll love Toyworld. They sell toys and games from major manufacturers at reduced prices. And they're the largest stockists of TP activity and outdoor toys in the North.
*Crown Point House, 110 Hunslet Lane, Leeds • 0113 222 3344*

### Woolworths
All the major brands are well represented here. You'll find Winnie the Pooh and friends, Barbie, Action Man

## Engage Your Senses
### The sights and sounds of Kirkgate Market
Shopping for children doesn't always have to mean visiting large superstores and high street chains. For a more sensory experience, why not take them to Kirkgate Market? There's so much happening, always buzzing with activity, it's noisy and busy. And it's full of lots of different experiences, from the gruesome sights and smells of butchers' row to the dazzling colours of the greengrocers' stalls. There are also plenty of stalls that cater for children. If they've a pet, you'll probably be interested in Tails Pet Shop where you can get most things needed to look after a small animal. And there's no doubt they'll be keen to visit Brown's Famous Sweet Shop, with chocolates and candies piled as high as the stall itself. However, you may be happier for them to spend their pocket money at Moore's Allsorts Confectionery — they specialise in sugar-free sweets. There's also The Toy Shop, Irene's Baby Boutique and Charisma — an accessories stall with plenty of inexpensive items that would make a great addition to any dressing-up box. What's more, by shopping in the market, you can generally expect to spend less than the high street prices. So not only is this a fun way to shop, it's also inexpensive.

Kirkgate Market

and the latest Disney/Pixar merchandise, as well as pocket money toys, outdoor items and even some bikes. A real something for everyone place. Convenient too, as they also stock a wide range of videos aimed at children. Cleverly, they keep the games consoles in a separate department. And that's because Playstation's for grown ups. We don't want you children getting funny ideas. It's ours. Oh, and I challenge you to go into Woolworths and not buy a huge bag of pick 'n' mix.

*White Rose Shopping Centre, Leeds • 0113 277 6823*

## Kids' Clothes

**Kids grow out of clothes quicker than you can buy them; but paper bags will never be in fashion, so try a few of these for size.**

### Adams Childrenswear

It's clear they understand the stresses and strains kids put onto their clothes: everything is highly practical and easy to wash and dry. They try to make life easier too by creating trousers for the newly potty-trained that aren't hard to remove and put back on the right way round! Boys' clothes are fashionable without using the embarrassing colours and designs that Mum may love but he's guaranteed to hate. For girls they offer mix and match, up-to-date looks that they'll love creating outfits from.

*22-26 The Headrow, Leeds • 0113 2448907*

### Boodle Am

If you're looking for a pair of Kickers, this is the place to come. From a pair of 'My First Kickers' all the way up to larger sizes, they've the whole spectrum of colours. And they've even got Twister Laces to go with them.

*27-29 County Arcade, Victoria Quarter, Leeds • 0113 245 8220*

### Clarks Shoes

For years, they've been the first choice for children's shoes. And that's because they know that to really look after your child's foot, a shoe doesn't just to have to fit well — it must be well made too. And high-quality attractive shoes are what they excel at.

*34 Commercial Street, Leeds • 0113 245 0339*

### Gap

From babies all the way up to teenagers, Gap offers fun, high quality clothing. So if you want to inject a bit of wholesome Americana into your family, this is the place to start. They've also great accessories, from hats to bags. And around back-to-school time, they've usually got some practical and stylish cool-bag style lunch boxes that are equally at home in your office as they are in the playground.

*135 Briggate, Leeds • 0113 243 9414*

### Mamas and Papas

Cute without being sickly, the newborn and baby clothes are a great example of their philosophy of style and fashion, blended with comfort and safety.

*Holden Ing Way, Gelderd Road, Birstall, Leeds • 0870 830 7707*

### New Look

If you've a surly 9-15 year-old girl, this is the place to bring her. They've all the latest looks translated into children's sizes so she'll be able to look cool — without it costing a fortune. Quality isn't exactly their strong point, but that's okay. It'll be 'out' before it falls apart.

*Unit Q 27 Albion Arcade, Leeds • 0113 234 2736*

### Next

As well as a range of clothes for children from newborn up to 16 years old, there's also a surprisingly affordable skiwear collection. So if you're planning a family holiday to a ski-destination, it's going to cost less than you think to kit everyone out.

*Unit 1, West Riding House, Albion Street, Leeds • 0113 200 1300*

### Start-Rite

You can rely on Start-Rite for stylish footwear from the first pair all the way through to early teens. Shoes are available in half sizes and up to six width fittings to offer gentle support, especially designed to care for feet as they grow. They also have Barbie and Action Man trainers.

*Within Debenhams, White Rose Centre, Leeds • 0113 270 7550*

### Wickid

Providing high fashion and functional clothing for all children from the ages of 0 to 10 years, their collection includes pretty dresses, fun & functional separates, hats, scarves, matching tights, coats, jackets and quality designs for all occasions. Brands include Trussardi, Emile et Rose, IKKS, and Marese.

*79 New Road Side, Horsforth, Leeds • 0113 258 7171*

*Mamas & Papas*

## Fancy Dress and Party Accessories

All you need to make your party go with a bang, or to disguise yourself at the next Parents' Evening.

### Bagged & Bowed

Offering a choice of up to 10 designs for boys' and girls' party bags.
*26 Kingsley Crescent, Birkenshaw, Bradford • 01274 869 345*

### Bash

Everything you'll need in one shop — balloons, fireworks and other party goods.
*94 Street Lane, Roundhay, Leeds • 0113 266 9191*

### Fancy Dress Experience

As well as a wide range of costumes, including some for couples who want to dress as a double act, they have fireworks all year round.
*13b North Lane, Headingley, Leeds • 0113 230 4700*

### Homburgs

With over 30,000 costumes to choose from, it's a good job they've over 50 years' experience — you're going to need some help choosing! They've pretty much everything you can think of plus some great ideas you didn't.
*King House, Regent Street, Leeds • 0113 245 8425*

### Pink Banana

Don't even think of going anywhere else if you're planning a birthday party. They've everything you need. Pick 'n' mix and small toys to go in party bags, the essential paper plates and cups to prevent breakage (and washing up). They'll even fill helium balloons for you. Of course, they also stock toys and it's quite a diverse selection, from *Monsters inc* and *Star Wars* merchandise to plastic jewellery sets and water pistols.
*8 Regent Street, Chapel Allerton, Leeds • 0113 269 6136*

### Sandroy Fancy Dress Hire

Spread over three floors are over 2000 costumes. They've a specialist children's and teenagers' department and all the accessories, wigs and make up you need to go with their costume.
*74 Cross Gates Road, Leeds • 0113 232 8123*

### The Loony Bin

An excellent range of costumes for adults and children, as well as enough wigs, masks, balloons, magic, jokes and face paints to make any party go with a bang!
*100 Town Street, Armley, Leeds • 0113 279 5350*

## Babygear

Make sure you're well-equipped for when Mr Stork comes a-calling.

### Baby Centre

Stocking an enormous range of prams, cots, high chairs, car seats and pushchairs, you'll find quality brands such as Bebecar, Britax, Bertini, Chicco, Maclaren, and Silver Cross. There are also over 20 bedroom displays showing off a variety of furniture and accessories.
*Mam House, 91 Roseville Road, Leeds • 0113 2455 680*

### baby d

A department store for 0-10 year olds, it stocks one of the north's largest ranges of nursery and bedroom furniture, prams, car seats, bedding, and fine gifts.
*Cheltenham Mount, Harrogate • 0800 389 2869*

### Baby Direct

If you're thinking of taking your child 'off road', you'll be interested in their all terrain buggies. And if you're really serious about it, it's likely you'll quickly be taking advantage of their repair and valet service too. Also stock christening wear.
*96 New Road Side, Leeds • 0800 026 9373*

Shopping Guide

*Out Now!*

shopping in Leeds made easy

Available from all good newsagents and book stores or call direct 0113 244 1000

**THE LEEDS GUIDE**

### Babyscene

With a 4000 square foot showroom, they've a wide range of baby and nursery products all under one roof. They're also a Mamas & Papas premier stockist and a Silver Cross Heritage Centre.
*Bradford Road, Keighley • 01535 681 021*

### Guiseley Pram & Nursery Store

In addition to a wide range of prams, cots and travel equipment from brands such as Cosatto, Bebecar, and Maxi-cosi, they also offer a car seat fitting service from Britax trained staff.
*West Side Retail Park, Guiseley • 01943 870 950*

### Mamas and Papas

This company was born from the frustration of not being able to find products that were both practical and stylish. Providing prams and pushchairs, nursery furniture and equipment, maternity and babywear through to toys and rocking horses. Their philosophy of style and fashion, blended with comfort and safety, creates exciting ideas and designs.
*Holden Ing Way, Gelderd Road, Birstall, Leeds • 0870 830 7707*
*Colne Bridge Road, Huddersfield, 01484 438 200*

### Mothercare

Mothercare have been around so long, you probably slept/ate/played in a Mothercare product. Fortunately, they've moved with the times so you'll find a modern choice in everything from the dream nursery to the safest car seats. Advisors are well-trained and can answer questions about a child's needs at all levels of development. They also hold in-store classes and discussion groups.
*1 Albion Arcade, Bond Street Centre, Leeds • 0113 243 8927*
*White Rose Centre, Millshaw Road, Leeds • 0113 271 2778*
*Victoria Garden Shopping Centre, Station Parade, Harrogate • 01423 561 265*
*36 Princess Alexandra Walk, Huddersfield • 01484 426 490*
*Crown Point Retail Park Junction St, Leeds • 0113 244 0555*

### Toys R Us

The Babies 'R' Us department provides furniture, car seats, bedding, strollers, safety products, nappies and baby food, and advisors are highly trained in all aspects of babycare, to ensure that they can offer the best service and advice to parents and parents-to-be. Open seven days-a-week, they have free parking, baby changing facilities and helpful staff — so much so that they've won the Tommy Most Parent Friendly Award for the last six years running. *Gelderd Road, Birstall, Batley, West Yorkshire • 01924 420 556*
*Unit 1, Westgate Retail & Leisure Park, Wakefield • 01924 200 884*

During your visit to the Royal Armouries you'll find it hard to walk past the museum shop without being drawn in by the treasures on display. What better way to end your trip than to take home a little piece of the Armouries for yourself? As well as the gifts and books you would expect to find, you'll be surprised by some of the other items on offer, such as replica swords and armours.

Why not settle down in the reading corner to browse through the broad range of books and videos for the arms and military enthusiast including the Royal Armouries' own publications.

The shop also carries a range of stylish homewares including vases, candles and frames inspired by some of the Collection's more ornate pieces. A special section dedicated to younger visitors contains books and pocket money toys plus accessories such as swords and medieval costumes to fire the imaginations of 'mini maidens' and 'small squires'.

Theatres, Cinemas & Concerts

*Carnival Messiah at West Yorkshire Playhouse*

Theatre is only for grown-ups ... OH NO IT'S NOT!!! Oh, okay, then. As well as seasonal family fun with pantos, many theatres have an eye on getting kiddie-sized behinds on seats all year round. Cinemas, meanwhile, are bringing magic back to Saturday mornings whilst the region's concert halls frequently have something of interest to young ears.

## Theatres

### Alhambra Studio Theatre

Hosts kids events to accompany shows in the main theatre, like *The Firebird* and *Spooky Tales* and new and exciting drama for young people, like CHOL Theatre's *The Ghost Lesson*.
*Entrance in Great Horton Road, Bradford • 01274 752 000*

### Alhambra Theatre

This venue is a splendidly regal night out with its ornate design and grand stage, without being alienating or stuffy. Many of their recent productions have been family favourites, from *Fame* to *Forbidden Planet*, *Grease* to *Joseph & the Technicolour Dreamcoat* as well as visits from the wonderful Sooty and Postman Pat and a plethora of pantos.
*Morley Street, Bradford • 01274 752 000*

Grand Theatre

### Grand Theatre & Opera House

Definitely Leeds' classiest and most elegant venue: you will find shows for toddlers — *The Wheels on the Bus* where you can sing along to your favourite nursery rhymes (or at least the kids can, you can always wait in the bar) — or for young adults, an introduction to the rarefied delights of Mozart's *The Magic Flute* (they won't be disappointed) and the Moscow City Ballet's *Sleeping Beauty* and *Nutcracker*, the pinnacle of modern ballet.
*46 New Briggate, Leeds • 0113 222 6222*

*The Borrowers at West Yorkshire Playhouse*

### Lawrence Batley Theatre

A lively programme with its own youth theatre group and an annual LEAP Festival of Dance and Drama with professional companies alongside school and community groups. Productions include *The Wizard of Oz* (and what child wouldn't love to follow the yellow brick road?) and *Around the World in Eighty Days*.
*Queen's Square, Huddersfield* • *01484 430 528*

### Leeds City Varieties Music Hall

Occasional family shows like *The Wiz*, a contemporary reworking of Dorothy's adventures in Oz with rock, gospel and soul. You could always take the kids to *The Good Old Days* but I'm not sure if they'd thank you. The venue itself is a visual treat, full of plush red Victoriana and gilding.
*Swan Street, Leeds* • *0113 243 0808*

### Leeds Civic Theatre

Probably the strongest programme for kids in the region with the all-singing-all-dancing *Guys & Dolls*, the ultra-accessible Shakespeare 4 Kidz' *Macbeth* and *A Midsummer Night's Dream*, the space age musical adventure *The Kosmic Crew* and the old chestnuts *Rumpelstiltskin, Jack & the Beanstalk* and, in the New Year, *Snow White*.
*Cookridge Street, Leeds* • *0113 214 5315*

### Viaduct Theatre

Don't be put off by the dark, dank prospect of this subterranean theatre space in a former textile mill. This is the perfect place to introduce your coming-of-age offspring to the wonders of Shakespeare and the classics from a gritty northern perspective. Barrie Rutter's company, Northern Broadsides, takes the work of Jacobean and Greek masters and transforms them into a wonderfully accessible pot pourri of Yorkshire vernacular, physicality and innovative design. Also based here are IOU Theatre whose *Cure* and *Tattoo* reach out to a young audience with an endearing wit and great sense of spectacle.
*Dean Clough, Halifax*

### Victoria Theatre

Fe, fo, fi, fum, it's panto-tastic with *Jack & the Beanstalk* and a selection of vintage stars and whacky comedy.
*Ward's End, Halifax* • *01422 351 158*

### Wakefield Theatre Royal & Opera House

As well as being hot on the panto front — this year's Christmas treat is *Dick Whittington & His Cat* ("Oh, no, it isn't!") — this venue (easily accessible by train from Leeds) host dance extravaganzas such as *Movie Dance!* and youth productions like *Cinderella Jones*, a 21st-

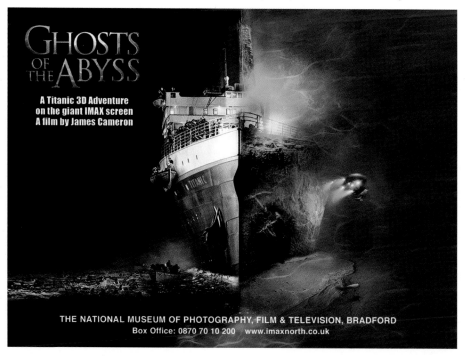

GHOSTS OF THE ABYSS

A Titanic 3D Adventure on the giant IMAX screen
A film by James Cameron

THE NATIONAL MUSEUM OF PHOTOGRAPHY, FILM & TELEVISION, BRADFORD
Box Office: 0870 70 10 200   www.imaxnorth.co.uk

## THE GRAND
### Theatre & Opera House, Leeds

## KIDS GUIDE

# Snow White
## and the
# Seven Dwarfs

**Mon 28 -
Wed 30 July**

Tickets: £7 - £8.50

DISCOUNTS AVAILABLE

**Holiday panto for all the family!**

# The Wheels on the BUS™

**THU 31 JULY -
SAT 2 AUG**

£7.00 - £8.50

DISCOUNTS AVAILABLE

Nursery Rhyme Time

BEEP

**BOX OFFICE 0113 222 6 222**

email: BoxOffice@lgt.demon.co.uk   www.leeds.gov.uk/GrandTheatre

*Little Shop of Horrors at West Yorkshire Playhouse*

century take on the classic fairy tale by local primary schools.

*Drury Lane, Wakefield* • *01924 211 311*

### West Yorkshire Playhouse

It's official: the WYP is the most accessible, innovative and creative venue in the region. The forthcoming season holds such theatrical delights as the Northern Ballet Theatre's *A Midsummer Night's Dream* (the most magical of Shakespeare's plays adapted for the north's premier ballet company), Kneehigh Theatre's *Cry Wolf!*, the Shakespeare School's Festival and, of course, the lovely panto *The Elves & the Shoemaker*.

*Playhouse Square, Quarry Hill, Leeds* • *0113 213 7700*

## Cinemas

When the weather is nasty (which, let's face it, is pretty much most of the time) and the allure of watching the same Disney movie on DVD for the 500th time is waning, take your little darlings to experience the movies in all its full screen glory.

There used to be a time when cinemas bent over backwards to cater for children. Remember the days of the Saturday matinee? A cartoon, followed by an episodic serial from the 30s ('Flash Gordon' was always the best), then a deathly dull documentary (often narrated by John 'Blue Peter' Noakes) and, finally, the main feature itself. Add all the Kia-Ora and sweets your pocket money could stretch to, and the children had a great time ... and the adults had a quiet afternoon.

Whilst those days are long gone, there are still plenty of opportunities for your children to enjoy the magic of the moving image. The Hyde Park Picture House keeps the tradition of the Saturday matinee alive. Whilst the serials and documentaries are sadly absent, the admission is an extremely reasonable 20p and, with a mixture of new releases and children's classics, it should keep everyone entertained. The Hebden Bridge Picture House also runs a Kids' Club every other Saturday. With fun and activities before the film, and the chance to join the Kids' Club for £5 (you get a free ticket to a Kids Club Film, plus a membership card, badge and newsletter amongst other cool things), it beats renting a video. City Screen in York also offer a Kids' Club every Saturday, with the requisite games and fun.

The multiplexes also do their bit for looking after the youngsters. Warner Village offers The Cinemaniacs Club which offers discounts on films, competitions and lots of fun games and activities. To join, go to www.cinemaniacs.co.uk for all the information. Ster Century Cinemas also offer a Weekly Kids Club with discounts on some of the best new movies. The Odeon and Showcase cinemas don't have a dedicated Kids Club, but they still do offer good discounts and plenty of fun in between watching the latest releases.

The National Museum of Photography, Film and Television not only offers a great interactive experience but offers special education events and screenings. The perfect place for your kids to use the cinema as a learning tool, the museum also holds the Bradford Animation Festival every November. Whilst often aimed at industry professionals, there is still lots here for your kids to enjoy. Speaking of festivals, the Leeds Children's and Young Persons Film Festival offers a great selection of films from around the world during March and April. With workshops, events and a chance for children to get involved with the actual running of the festival, it shows there's more to life than Disney.

With events, workshops, games and — of course — films, there's so much on offer. Still, people are still missing out on episodes of 'Flash Gordon'. Well, you can't have everything ...

All prices and Kids' Club offers and times are subject to change. Please check with relevant cinema before booking. All Kids Ticket prices quoted below do not take into account Kids' Club special offers.

### City Screen
*Coney Street, York • 01904 541 144 • www.picture-house-cinemas.co.uk • Children £3.50*

### Hebden Bridge Picture House
*New Road, Hebden Bridge • 01422 842807 • www.hebdenbridge-picturehouse.co.uk • Children £2.50*

Warner Village

**IT'S GOING TO BE A LONG, BLOCKBUSTING SUMMER ...**

June:
BRUCE ALMIGHTY

July:
CHARLIE'S ANGELS 2: HALO
THE HULK

August:
TERMINATOR 3: RISE OF THE MACHINES

Critic's choice film:
Every Wed. at 8.15pm

**MAKE SURE YOU ENJOY IT ALL ON OUR BIGGER SCREENS**

**STER CENTURY**
CINEMAS
**LEEDS' ONLY CITY CENTRE CINEMA**

**Book Online at**
**www.stercentury.co.uk**
**or call the Box Office on**
**0870 240 3696**

Ster Century Cinemas, The Light,
The Headrow, Leeds

*13 Big Screens, Better Sound, Comfier Seats, More Legroom*

### Hyde Park Picture House
*Brudenell Road, Hyde Park, Leeds • 0113 275 2045 • www.leedscinema.com • Children £2.8*

### National Museum of Photography, Film and Television
*Pictureville, Bradford • 0870 70 10 200 • www.nmpft.org.uk • Children £4.20 (Imax), £2.50 (Cinemas, before 4.30pm), £3.30 (Cinemas, after 4.30pm)*

### Odeon Cinema
*Gallagher Leisure Park, Thornbury, Bradford • 0870 5050007 • www.odeon.co.uk • Children £3.70*

### Showcase Cinemas
*Gelderd Road, Birstall • 01924 423 000 • www.showcasecinemas.co.uk • Children £4 (Tues) £4.20 (All Other Days)*

### Ster Century
*The Headrow, Leeds • 0870 240 3696 • www.stercentury.co.uk • Children £4*

### Warner Village
*Cardigan Fields Leisure Park, Kirkstall Road, Leeds • 08702 40 60 20 • www.warnervillage.co.uk • Children £3.90*

Hyde Park Picture House

Ster Century

# SATURDAY KIDS' MATINEES
## AT THE hyde park
PICTURE HOUSE

ALL CHILDREN'S ADMISSIONS 20p ONLY

**EVERY SATURDAY AT 12noon**
**check www.leedscinema.com for listings**
**OR CALL THE CINEMA ON 0113 275 2045**
Hyde Park Picture House, Brudenell Road, Headingley, Leeds, LS6 1JD

Don't miss The Kids' Guide
2004/05 edition out June 2004.

If you want to be included in next year's guide
please contact the Kids Guide editor on 0113 244 1000.

THE LEEDS GUIDE

## Music to your Ears

### Concerts that are music to parents' ears

Many venues such as Leeds City Varieties and St George's Hall in Bradford have pop concerts aimed at kids — often tributes to current top 40 acts, or sometimes the acts themselves. However, those wishing to introduce their children to classical music may feel daunted by the prospect of three-hour operas and 'difficult' modern composition instilling a lifelong fear in the young concert-goer.

With that in mind, Leeds International Concert Season has special family concerts dotted throughout the year. 2003's line-up is as varied as ever. The first concert is an appearance by the athletic Mugenkyo Taiko Drummers, who beat out powerful rhythms on huge, pounding drums with impressive grace. Next comes two musical puppet shows: *Spud Pirate and the Pot of Gold* — which follows shy hero Spud on a seafaring adventure — and *The Firebird*, a fairytale story of sturdy heroes and fearsome villains.

Finally, there's *The Flying Recorder*: covering seven centuries of recorder music on 15 different types of recorder — with the chance to bring your own along and join in with some pieces — it should inspire even the most reluctant learners of that staple of school music lessons.

Many of the season's other concerts are also suitable for the family, including a Christmas Carol show and appearances by brass bands in the city's parks on Sundays.

19 October **Mugenkyo Taiko Drummers**

23 November **Spud Pirate and the Pot of Gold**

25 January 2004 **The Firebird**

29 February 2004 **The Flying Recorder**

*Leeds International Concert Season* • *0113 247 8336*

Eating & Drinking

Courtesy of the Lounge at Radisson

# Eating & Drinking

## Child-Friendly Restaurants

Having kids doesn't have to mean a life-sentence down your local burger joint. These establishments welcome diners of all ages, and they don't all have Formica tables and wipe-clean walls.

### Bar 88

An international cuisine restaurant that enables you to travel the four corners of the globe, occasionally on the same plate. Vietnamese spring rolls and seafood Japanese noodles mix happily with satays, pork fillets and mixed grill or even a burger and chips. If you can get your head around the chef's shocking disregard for international boundaries you'll thoroughly enjoy yourself.
*17 Eastgate, Leeds • 0113 225 6622 • Highchair, Pushchair Access*

### Bella Pasta

About as authentically Italian as a Cornetto it may be, but the UK's largest pasta chain has a reasonably-priced, reliable selection of pasta and pizzas nevertheless. The staff are usually attentive and enthusiastic, whilst if you fancy the prospect of Briggate in mid-summer then there's an outside café section.
*145 Briggate, Leeds • 0113 245 4630 • Children's menu £3.95 • Vegetarian friendly, Bottle-heating, Highchair, Pushchair Access*

### Betty's Café Tearooms

The Harrods of tearooms. With cakes that give you a sugar rush just by looking at them, eating in Betty's is an expensive treat. Paradise for kids, and more work for their dentist. Be prepared to queue before they can stuff themselves with a formidable Fat Rascal while you refuel with one of the potent speciality coffees.
*1 Parliament Street, Harrogate • 01423 502 746 • Vegetarian friendly, Bottle-heating, Highchair*

### Bistro Fiori

Situated in the heart of the Central Business District, Bistro Fiori is usually busy, and is popular with afternoon and evening diners alike. However, its Tardis-like interior and high standard of service allow enough space in which to enjoy the tempting Italian food.
*8 Commercial Street, Leeds • 0113 243 8280 • Children's Menu £4.95. • Bottle-heating, Highchair*

### Bretts

Forget greasy newspaper, Bretts take plain old fish 'n' chips to gourmet level. There are a range of starters like breaded lobster tails but, as the menu cheekily asserts, the main course is what really brings 'em in. There's not much on offer for those who don't like fish but for those who do — why then the world's your

Betty's Café Tearooms

oyster. Or haddock, or plaice, or anything you care to think of.
*12-14 North Lane, Headingley, Leeds • 0113 232 3344 • Children's menu £3.20 • Vegetarian friendly, Highchair*

### Browns Restaurant

Browns provides elegance without the 'do not touch' factor; it's an under-the-top study in 'classic', being all plants, air, open spaces, dim lights, leather and wood. The menu mimics this mood, with comfortable dishes that while unchallenging, aren't boring either. Elevated pastas, salads, burgers and steaks are ordered alongside indulgent milk shakes, garlic breads, and hot fudge brownies.
*The Light, Permanent House 70-72, The Headrow, Leeds • 0113 243 9353 • Children's menu £3.95 • Vegetarian friendly, Bottle-heating, Highchair, Pushchair Access*

### Bryans

A good old Yorkshire fish 'n' chip restaurant, tucked away just off the Otley Road, and with the feel of a cottage living room, down to the framed and signed photos of 'Emmerdale' luvvies. Portions are mountainous and melt-in-the-mouth fish is coated with a perfect, crispy batter.
*9 Weetwood Lane, Leeds • 0113 278 5679 • Vegetarian friendly, Bottle-heating, Highchair, Pushchair Access*

### Cactus Lounge

Making surprisingly good use of what seems a small space, Cactus Lounge is a cosy haven for Mexican food like burritos, enchiladas and fajitas and excellently located for pre-theatre food. Fajitas or the pescado are good choices, as is the sticky toffee pud which is excellent comfort food.
*Yorkshire Dance Centre, 3 St Peters Square, Leeds • 0113 243 6553 • Bottle-heating, Half portions, Highchair*

### Café Rouge

As one of those established 'Big Business Brand Name' type places, Café Rouge is one of the classiest. The French art deco lights, sofas and fittings attract young professionals for a first civilised tipple on a night out that will get messier later on but during the day it's more than suitable for the family.

*Waterloo House, Assembly Street, Leeds • 0113 245 1551 • Children's menu £3.95-£6.95 •Bottle-heating, Highchair*

## Calls Grill

One of the Calls' many upmarket eateries, Calls Grill sports an airy interior done out with brick and timber regeneration chic. An attractive environment in which to tarry whilst your gut languishes in the opulent, diet-busting menu. There's an emphasis on seafood (for example tempura battered salmon fingers with pan-scorched oriental veg) and steak, with a choice of cuts and cooking times on offer with kid's choices too.

*36-38 The Calls, Leeds • 0113 245 3870 • Children's menu £3 • Bottle-heating, Highchair, Pushchair Access*

## Casa Mia

Part of a duo of Italian restaurants owned by the hyper-friendly and hard-working husband and wife team Francesco and Marta. This one specializes in fish dishes which come fresh with delicate sauces. Also recommended is the vegetarian antipasto. The atmosphere is jovial and holiday-like.

*10 Stainbeck Lane, Chapel Allerton, Leeds • 0113 266 1269 • Vegetarian friendly, Half portions*

## Cinnamon Room

First floor restaurant with glass walls allowing you to bathe in the jealous looks of the hungry masses below. Fortunately, the food more than meets the standards set by the surroundings. This is top class Indian fare with plenty of mild options for the wee ones. Impressive location, excellent food and all for an absolute steal — once tried you'll find it difficult to eat a curry anywhere else without being massively disappointed.

*34 Oxford Street, Harrogate • 01423 505 300 • Bottle-heating, Half portions, Highchair*

## Clock Café

The Clock Café is nicely laid-back. The loungey soundtracks combine with the wooden floor and the lively yellows and blues to give the impression of a convivial country kitchen. The menu is predominantly Mediterranean and priced to accommodate the student wallet, meaning good value for those with little ones too.

*16a Headingley Lane, Hyde Park Corner, Leeds • 0113 294 5464 • Vegetarian friendly, Half portions*

## Corn Mill Lodge Hotel

The Corn Mill Lodge Hotel is used primarily by tourists seeking a base from which to visit the various

MEDITERRANEAN RESTAURANT

Dimitri's

TAPAS BAR

Healthy eating for kids

SIMPSONS FOLD, DOCK STREET , LEEDS
T: 0113 246 0339   F: 0113 246 0338
E: leeds@dimitris.co.uk   www.dimitris.co.uk

Dimitri's

attractions that good old Yorkshire has to offer. It also features a brasserie, Le Continental, which is open to non-residents.

*Pudsey Road, Leeds • 0113 257 9059 • Vegetarian friendly, Bottle-heating, Highchair, Pushchair Access*

### Cutlers Bar & Brasserie

The menu is exotic without turning its back on British culinary elements - poached egg florentine, grilled sweet baby black pudding and an army of assorted pastry boxes. The philosophy here is of building meals out of interesting starters - such that any item may be ordered as a starter or main.

*Main Street, Burley in Wharfedale • 01943 862 207 • Children's menu £3.75-£5.25. • Bottle-heating, Highchair, Pushchair Access*

### Darbar

Wildly exotic-looking restaurant that'll have you singing Bollywood style and dancing on tables if the food doesn't prove enough of a distraction; which it probably will. An extensive specialities menu offers up some awesomely tasty dishes. The service, meanwhile, is swift, attentive and professional: the chef sometimes comes out to greet the diners, and occasionally gives out gifts like a white-behatted Santa.

*16-17 Kirkgate, Leeds • 0113 246 0381 • Bottle-heating, Half portions, Highchair*

### Dimitri's

Although Dimitri's is a resident of Leeds' breathlessly fashionable riverside quarter, its identity is firmly rooted in the dry soil of Greece. Dishes to look out for include their Skordalia (a walnut and garlic dip) and Keftedes (lamb meatballs with tomato sauce). Parties can share the mezes (or the mega version), with an array of dips, tapas and pitta bread with a meaty, seafood or vegetarian theme.

*24-26 Dock Street, Leeds • 0113 246 0339 • Bottle-heating, Half portions, Highchair*

### Garden Brasserie

Restaurant nestled in one of the newest hotels in the city with styling that matches the modern look synonymous with city living. The menu is varied: from the dish of the day, full meals or light snacks to à la carte menus.

*Novotel Leeds Centre, 4 Whitehall, Whitehall Quay, Leeds • 0113 242 6446 • Children's menu £3.95 • Bottle-heating, Highchair, Play room*

### Hard Rock Cafe

Now that HRC have more than proved themselves as the fore-runners of globalisation, it seems a city is not a city without a Hard Rock. Situated in the booming Cube complex, Hard Rock Leeds offer all the wonderfully indulgent American diner fodder we the people and — more importantly — the kids demand, like New York strip steaks, speciality burgers and stupidly delicious ice-cream shakes.

*The Cube, Albion Street, Leeds • 0113 200 1310 • Vegetarian friendly, Bottle-heating, Highchair, Pushchair Access*

### Harry Ramsdens

Justly famous fish and chip emporium, this is more than just a restaurant, it's a tourist attraction: the first of the famous Harry Ramsden's now colonising the chips and batter world. It now has a grill serving a wide variety of meat and fish including swordfish and chicken.

*White Cross, Guiseley • 01943 874 641 • Vegetarian friendly, Highchair, Pushchair Access*

### Harvey Nichols Fourth Floor Cafe & Bar

Stylish bar, although you do have to navigate the shop itself to get there. As you'd expect from Harvey Nics, the drinks aren't cheap, the atmosphere is civilised, food servings are generous and service is impeccable. Still even the stylish set have children, and they're more than welcome here (although you may feel under pressure to dress them in the very latest kid's clothes).

*107 Briggate, Leeds • 0113 204 8888 • Vegetarian friendly, Bottle-heating, Highchair, Pushchair Access*

### Henrys Cafe Bar

Easygoing and reliable café bar, which provides a good lunch stop for office works in the business quarter but with kiddie options too.

*10 Greek Street, Leeds • 0113 245 9424 • Half portions, Highchair*

### Italian Job

Bustling little Italian with the no-nonsense personality of a real pizzeria and the waterfront location is absolutely lovely.

*9-11 Bridge End, Leeds • 0113 242 0185 • Vegetarian friendly, Bottle-heating, Half portions, Highchair, Play room, Pushchair Access*

### Jinnah Leeds

Superior Indian restaurant with the most boastful menu in Leeds: one item is described as "A classical Afghanistani dish [...] which considering the expense and efforts involved is normally cooked for royalty". The ambience is more diner than flock-house, and it is geared up well to cater for families. They will try to accommodate youngsters in any way possible.

*496 Roundhay Road, Oakwood, Leeds • 0113 240 9911 • Vegetarian friendly, Bottle-heating, Half portions, Highchair, Pushchair Access*

### Korks Wine Bar & Brasserie

Stylish wine bar housed in a building which — appropriately enough for the rural setting — used to sell farm equipment and machinery. The look is rustic sophistication: old tables and chairs emphasize Kork's distinctive character, whilst the long bar frames the main attraction — a grid of wine bins housing nearly 150 wines from around the world. Despite the booze-led nature of this place, it also caters for the children of its wine-loving clientele.

*40 Bondgate, Otley, Leeds • 01943 462 020 • Vegetarian friendly, Bottle-heating, Half portions, Highchair, Pushchair Access*

### La Comida

La Comida serves both Italian and Spanish food, although the former is more prominent in terms of the menu, which offers the usual range of pizzas and pasta. Nonetheless, there are a few token dishes from the Iberian region — notably the tapas, including such delights as liver pate and Parma ham.

*7/8 Mill Hill, Leeds • 0113 244 0500 • Bottle-heating, Half portions, Highchair, Pushchair Access*

### Leodis Brasserie

Part of Leeds' old guard and one of the prompts for the city's riverside rennaisance, this continental brasserie offers an impressively exotic menu, including the likes of oxtail and shin beef faggot, mash and girolle mushrooms but can also provide more appropriate dishes for children.

*Victoria Mill, Sovereign Street, Leeds • 0113 242 1010 • Bottle-heating, Half portions, Highchair, Pushchair Access*

### Livebait

Once used for rope-making, the airy brick interior now sports smart racing-green woodwork and black and white checked tiles, creating a homely yet efficient atmosphere that complements the fresh, carefully cooked fare and friendly, well-informed service who are well prepared for small people. Fish-lovers will be hooked.

*11-15 Wharf Street, The Calls, Leeds • 0113 244 4144 • Children's menu £5 • Bottle-heating, Highchair, Pushchair Access*

### MA Potters

Reasonably priced lunch diner or shopping stop-off with an imaginative menu, including the likes of chicken breast filled with ricotta cheese and basil served with chickpea cassoulet but, more importantly, a very large selection of children's menus.

*The Light, Leeds • 0113 246 1620 • Children's menu up to £3.65 • Vegetarian friendly, Bottle-heating, Highchair, Pushchair Access*

### Nandos

Family-oriented diner which specialises in flame grilled chicken accompanied by all sorts of sticky sauces and marinades. Try the sun-dried tomato and black olive or perhaps the extra hot 'peri-peri' if your mouth is lined with asbestos. Big portions, low prices.

*4 The Light, The Headrow, Leeds • 0113 242 8908 • Children's menu £3.95 • Bottle-heating, Highchair, Pushchair Access*

### No 3 York Place

Rechristened as No 3 York Place after the departure of top Leeds chef Simon Gueller, this restaurant has lost none of its brilliance despite the change of name and personnel. Service is efficient and attentive but not intrusive; all the better to concentrate on the supremely fine food. It's quite an extravagant affair but they are prepared to cater for children.

*3 York Place, Leeds • 0113 245 9922 • Bottle-heating, Half portions, Pushchair Access*

*Livebait*

# Eating & Drinking

## Olive Tree Restaurant

Inaugurated in 1986 and achieving the record for the world's longest kebab in 1990, the restaurant's faux marble pillars, soft lighting and candle-clasping statue of Aphrodite all hark back to the unsubtle interior chic of that heyday period. That said, the restaurant is popular, and rightly so, with its extensive menu of traditional Greek food.

*Oaklands, Rodley Lane, Rodley, Leeds • 0113 256 9283 • Children's menu £3.95 • Bottle-heating, Highchair, Pushchair Access*

## Paris Restaurant

French in inspiration, with a modern take on British cuisine, main courses are the likes of charred tuna, juicy venison and perfectly cooked lamb. Offers sumptuous desserts and a good vegetarian selection, in an airily spacious setting a world away from city bustle.

*Calverley Lane, Rodley, Leeds • 0113 258 1885 • Bottle-heating, Half portions, Highchair, Pushchair Access*

## Pizza Express

The ubiquitous upmarket pizza restaurant chain Pizza Express was founded by Peter Boizot back in 1965. Their open-plan premises share a friendly and relaxed atmosphere with a healthy clientele of families and couples plus the occasional 'Emmerdale' star who come to enjoy the classic American or the favoured Fiorentia. Kids can ask for mini-pizzas.

*Park House, Park Square West, Leeds • 0113 244 5858 • Vegetarian friendly, Bottle-heating, Half portions, Highchair, Pushchair Access*

## Roots & Fruits

With a mouth-watering array of international foods ranging from spinach and mushroom cannelloni and all-day veggie breakfast to plain old jacket spuds enlivened with myriad fillings and a sumptuous lemon cheesecake, Roots and Fruits fills the gap for veggies and sceptical meat-lovers alike who want quality munching with cafe informality.

*10-11 The Grand Arcade, Leeds • 0113 242 8313 • Bottle-heating, Half portions, Highchair, Pushchair Access*

## Sala-Thai

Sala Thai's marinades, pastes and sauces combine to make subtly complex dishes that succeed in not being overbearing, despite the rich ingredients — although the young ones may not be equipped to handle some of the spicier dishes. For starters, check out the daily hors d'oeuvres selection: spring rolls, wontons, beef and chicken satay and more.

*13-17 Shaw Lane, Headingley, Leeds • 0113 278 8400 • Vegetarian friendly, Bottle-heating, Half portions, Highchair, Pushchair Access*

## Salvos

Salvos is one of those permanently busy local restaurants that has no need for the force field of regenerate Leeds. They capably serve up high-end Italian classics with a family-run charm, and can easily cater for children.

*115 Otley Road, Headingley, Leeds • 0113 275 5017 • Children's menu £4.90 • Bottle-heating, Highchair, Pushchair Access*

## Shogun Teppanyaki

As if the sight of their food cooking right in front of them wasn't enough stimulation for your kids, there's an additional bonus — they can sit back and gawp as the chef juggles ingredients, dicing and slicing in mid-air as he works. The skill with which they perform their dazzling displays of dexterity will blow you all away, as will the outstanding food.

*Granary Wharf, Leeds • 0113 245 1856 • Children's menu up to £12.95 • Vegetarian friendly, Bottle-heating, Highchair, Pushchair Access*

## Simply Heathcotes

With Paul Heatcoate at the helm, the menu here is now exclusively British, offering unashamedly traditional fare such as fish and chips, roast ham and strawberries and cream.

*2 Canal Wharf, Leeds • 0113 244 6611 • Children's menu up to £6.99 • Bottle-heating, Pushchair Access*

## Tampopo

A restaurant where good value, fast service and reliable quality are achieved, the downside being that the menu rarely changes. The whole atmosphere is stylish but simple, with colourful art on the white walls and customers seated on long wooden benches like a school canteen. Tampopo is ideal for a speedy visit to stop stomachs rumbling during a day in town.

*15 South Parade, Leeds • 0113 245 1816 • Children's menu £3.95 • Bottle-heating, Highchair, Pushchair Access*

## TGI Friday

To be recommended if you feel that your food isn't authentically American without an extra topping of 'Hi guys!' cheese from the energetic staff. That said, it is great for kids, with an enormous selection of menus to suit different age ranges.

*City Gate, Wellington Street, Leeds • 0113 242 8103 • Children's menu £2.95-£7.75 • Bottle-heating, Highchair, Pushchair Access*

Clubs, Societies & Workshops

Courtesy of Leeds Leisure Services

# Clubs, Societies & Workshops

West Yorkshire is full of clubs and societies for young people: below is a selection of the larger groups. For older children, local councils can provide details of local youth clubs and organisations

## Societies

### Girlguiding

Over half of UK women have been a Brownie, a Guide or a Rainbow at some point in their lives and Girlguiding UK, as it is called nowdays, has done much to shed its image of brown bobble hats and cookery badges, with an emphasis on varied activities and self-development. Call 0800 169 5901 for details of your local group, or visit www.girlguiding.org.uk

### Scouting

The UK's most popular youth movement is now open to both boys and girls of all faiths (although those with no religion may feel a conflict with the movement's aims), offering friends, activities — plenty of which are of the outdoor type — and community awareness for all ages. Call 0845 300 1818 or visit www.scoutbase.org.uk for details and joining information.

### The Woodcraft Folk

Originally a breakaway from the Scouting movement, the Woodcraft Folk has a more overtly environmental and pacifist slant, aiming to build co-operation between children. Meetings involve games, drama and music, and hiking, hostelling and camping excursions during weekends or holidays, with a special camping centre based near Todmorden. Call 0845 458 9535 for details or visit www.poptel.org.uk/woodcraft

## Orchestras and Music

### Fun Music for Children

*20 Whitehall Croft, Rothwell, Leeds, 0113 282 0419*
Introducing children aged between one and nine to music.

### Jo Jingles

*7 Hill Estate, Upton, Pontefract, 01977 650 455*
Musical games for pre-school children. Meets in Garforth Leisure Centre on Wednesday mornings.

### Leeds Girls' Choir

*186 Street lane, Roundhay, Leeds, 0113 392 2406*
Meets Wednesday evenings at Leeds College of Music. For girls and women aged eight-21.

### Leeds Youth Opera

*426 Spen Lane, Leeds, 0113 267 4703*
Rehearsing and performing two operas per year as well as various local concerts/cabarets. Meets Saturday mornings at West Park Centre.

### Huddersfield Youth Brass Ensemble Association

*Golcar Conservative Club, Knowl Road, Golcar, Huddersfield*
Rehearsals on Tuesday evenings. Contact Alan Jazwinski on 01484 312920 for details

Photo by Colin White

The Woodcraft Folk

*Eureka!*

## Creative Activities

See Galleries section for details of gallery-run art activities.

### Eureka!

*Discovery Road, Halifax, 01422 330 012*

The hands-on science museum runs regular Saturday workshops where kids can make crafts inspired by current exhibitions or for occasions such as Easter, as well as making music and learning in a fun way.

### Young Writers' Group

*Huddersfield Library, Princess Alexandra Walk, Huddersfield, 01484 221 961*

Group for 15-19-year olds meeting on the first Monday of every month. Contact Sharon Allwood on 01484 226354 or Sharon.allwood@kirklees.gov.uk for details.

## Drama

### City Varieties Youth Theatre

*Leeds City Varieties Music Hall, Swan Street, Leeds, 0113 243 0808*

A chance for children aged between five and 14 to develop their theatre skills. Runs on Thursdays (eight-to-14s) and Saturdays (five-to-sevens) during termtime.

## Then I'll Begin...

**Run out of bedtime books? Take your kids to a storytime session and let someone else enchant their ears**

Most local libraries run free storytime sessions for pre-school or infant-age kids, usually followed by a craft activity such as mask-making or drawing which is related to what the children have just heard. Leeds' Central Lending Library's storytime is on Thursdays between 10.30am and 11.30am, whilst Bradford Central Library runs one on Saturdays at 11am and the many libraries of Kirklees all have varied sessions. Look out for extra events during the summer hols and during 'Libraries Live' month, which in 2003 took place in May.

Borders Books and Music on Leeds' Briggate also invite the kids to sit down and listen on Saturday mornings (at 11.30am) and whilst the Story Time Sundays for three-to-eight year-olds at Eureka! require payment of the admission charge, they make a good bonus feature to a visit to the museum and promise to be equally interactive.

Parents of bookworm kids shouldn't forget the annual Ilkley Literature festival, from 3-19 October 2003. A special kids-focussed weekend from 10-12 October includes visits from Jacqueline Wilson and Benjamin Zephaniah — be quick, as tickets should move nearly as fast as a new *Harry Potter* volume.

## Knights of The Royal Armouries

Why not become a Knight of the Royal Armouries by joining their special membership scheme? Annual subscriptions range from £18 for senior citizens/concessions to £50 for 'Family & Friends' membership. On joining the scheme members receive a unique selection of retail items, discount vouchers and regular updates on special events. In addition members receive free entry to all special events, monthly members evenings, free tokens for the crossbow/pistol range, 10% discount on purchases in the museum shop, invitations to previews of new exhibits/exhibitions, exclusive talks and handling sessions and competitions. For further details about membership or to request an application form please call the Membership Department on 0113 220 1810.

## Group Visits

The diversity of the Royal Armouries collections enables them to offer a wide range of visits for all groups, including hands-on practical activities, specialist lectures and tours, with fascinating objects, fine handling collections and team of highly-trained interpreters ready to bring the collection to life. So whether your interests lie in history, art, technology or craftsmanship, the Armouries have something to offer every group from Scouts to WIs. For further information please call the Group Bookings Officer on 0113 220 1888 who will be happy to help you plan your visit.

*Dance Rehearsals at WYP*

## Cragrats Drama Group

*Cragrats Mill, Dunford Road, Holmfirth, 01484 686 451*
Drama for ages seven to 16.

## Leeds Childrens' Theatre

*Leeds Civic Theatre, Cookridge Street, Leeds, 0113 214 5315, www.leeds-childrens-theatre.co.uk*
Popular group running drama workshops during termtime

## LBT Youth Theatre

*Lawrence Batley Theatre, Queen's Square, Queen Street, Huddersfield, 01484 430 528*
Informal theatre workshops for ages five to eight, nine to 12, 13-15 and 16-21.

## Leeds Children's Circus

*13 Hilton Place, Harehills, Leeds, 0113 262 2815*
Circus skills for inner-city kids. Tuesday evenings during term-time.

## Stagecoach Theatre Arts School

*Leeds Grammar School, Alwoodley Gates, Harrogate Road, Leeds, 0113 229 1552*
Runs after school on Fridays. Contact Annette Baldwin on 01937 520 540 for details.

# Dance Classes

## Yorkshire Dance Centre

*Yorkshire Dance Centre, St Peter's Buildings, St Peter's Square, Leeds, 0113 243 8765*
Apart from the large number of independent dance teacher in Leeds, the YDC runs Saturday classes for kids from 'tots' to 12 years. Called WUSU — 'Wake Up Start Up' — they provide a good alternative to sitting in front of the TV all weekend.

Sport

*Courtesy of Leeds Leisure Services*

Wasn't the summer great when you were a kid? No school and no homework, just lazily spending time with your mates for days that seemed to last *forever*. But now you work. Get over it. Leave the sunshine to be enjoyed by the youngsters who, just to rub it in, now have even *more* things to do during the day than you did, especially when it comes to sporting activities, both playing and watching.

## Sports to Play

Hopscotch, hula-hoop and kicking a ball against a wall - it's the simple things in life, hey? Whatever.

## BMX Riding

**Leeds BMX Club**
*12 Monkswood Walk, Seacroft, Leeds LS14 1DL • 0113 293 6370*

**Leeds BMX Club**
*Cemetery Road, Yeadon Tarn, Yeadon*

**Bradford BMX Track**
*Peel Park, Undercliffe, Bradford*

## Canoeing

**Robin Hood Water Sports**
*152 Leeds Road, Heckmonwike, WF16 9BJ • 01924 444888*
Learn up to one star grade with a fully qualified instructor.

## Climbing

**Leeds Wall**
*100a Gelderd Road, Leeds LS12 6BY • 0113 234 1554*
Offers a range of courses as well as taster sessions for both adults and children.

## Football

**Skylark Leisure**
*1 Benson Parkway, Leeds LS12 6DP • 0113 383 3020*
Five-a-side and coaching.

## Golf Driving Ranges

**Walton Golf Centre**
*Common Lane Walton, Wakefield WF2 6PS • 01924 253 155*

**Ghyllbeck Golf Driving Range Ltd**
*Shot Lane, Basildon, Shipley BD17 7RJ • 01274 530 338*

## Horse-Riding

**Acre Cliff Riding School & Equestrian Centre**
*Eller Hill, Bradford Road, Otley LS21 3DN • 01943 873 912*

**Astley Riding School**
*Home Farm, Swillington, Leeds LS26 8UA • 0113 287 3078*

The Leeds Wall

*Ice Cube*

**Bankhouse Farm Riding & Livery Centre,**
*Wood Land, Middlestown, Wakefield WF4 4XD* • *01924 840 614*

**Cherry Tree Livery Stables,**
*Gill Lane, Kearby, Wetherby LS22 4BS* • *0113 288 6460*

**Follifoot Park Riding Centre**
*Pannal Road, Follifoot, Harrogate HG3 1DL* • *01423 870 372*

**Low Fold Equestrian**
*Low Fold Farm, Green Balk Lane, Little Lepton, Huddersfield HD8 0EW* • *01484 604 472*

**Middleton Park Equestrian Centre**
*Middleton Grove, Off Dewsbury Road, Leeds LS11 5TZ* • *0113 277 1962*

**Northern Riding and Carriage Drive Centre**
*The Stables, Water Lane, Thornhill Road, Dewsbury WF12 9PY* • *01924 466 240*

**Throstle Nest Riding School,**
*Throstle Nest Farm, Fagley Lane, Bradford BD2 3NU* • *01274 639 390*

**Wadlands Hall Equestrian Centre**
*Priesthorpe Road, Farsley, Pudsey LS28 5RD* • *0113 236 3648*

**Westways Riding School**
*The Homestead, Carr Lane, Thorner, Leeds LS14 3HD* • *0113 289 2598*

## Ice-Skating

**Bradford Ice Arena**
19 Little Horton Lane, Bradford, BD5 0AD • 01274 729 091

**Ice Cube**
Millennium Square, Leeds LS1 3DA • 0113 224 3600 Temporary ice-rink running Jan-Feb. Next one is 16 Jan-29 Feb 2004.

## Karting

**Anderson CSK Motorsport**
*Unit 2 Sterling Industrial Park, Carr Wood Road, Castleford WF10 4PS* • *01977 603 838*

**F1 Indoor Karting Ltd**
*Unit 5 Millennia Park, Thomas Road, Wakefield WF2 8PW* • *01924 201 808*

**Kart Skill**
*Riverside Raceway, South Accommodation Road, Leeds LS9 9AS* • *0113 249 1000*

**Leeds Bradford Karting**
*Fountain Works, Huddersfield Road, Roberttown, Liversedge, WF15 7QQ* • *01924 400 800*

**RS Karting Bradford Ltd**
*Springmill Street, Bradford BD5 7EE* • *01274 309 455*

## Martial Arts

**Bradford Aikido Club**
*Richard Dunn Sports Centre, Rooley Avenue, Odsal, BD6 1EZ • 01274 307 822*

**Bradford Bushido Ryu Shotokan Karate Club**
*Northcote Conservative Club, Undercliffe, Bradford • 01274 637 584*

**Ilkley Karate Club**
*Ben Rhydding Methodist Church, The Drive, Ilkley • 01943 601 297*

**Leeds Martial Arts College**
*Little Lane, Morley • 07831 303 093*

## Sailing

**Halifax Sailing Club,**
*14, Glen Mount Close, Wheatley, Halifax HX3 5AU*

**Huddersfield Sailing Club**
*Boshaw Whams Reservoir, Strines Moor Road, Hade Edge, Holmfirth, HD7 1RS*

**West Riding Sailing Club**
*Wintersett, Crofton, Wakefield WF4 2EE • 01924 863 617*

**Yeadon Sailing Club**
*Yeadon Tarn, Leeds • 0113 239 1258*

## Scuba-Diving

**Midway Watersports and Leisure**
*Main Street, Morley, Leeds • 0113 238 1500*
Robin Hood Dive School
*152 Leeds Road, Heckmondwike WF16 9BJ • 01924 443 843*

**Scuba Expeditions**
*Unit P, Granary Wharf, Neville Street, Leeds LS1 4BE • 0113 244 4316*

**Freedom Divers**
*376 Kirkstall Road, Leeds LS4 2HQ • 0113 368 2828*

## Skate Parks

**Aggro Vert**
*Unit 54, Calser Wharf Mills, Huddersfield Road, Ravensthorpe, Dewsbury WF13 3JW • 01924 439 439*

**Horsforth Hall Park**
*Hall Park, Ring Rd, Leeds LS18 4EL*

*Karting*

Photo by Chris Fell

## Roller Skating

**East Leeds Leisure Centre**
*Neville Road, Leeds LS15 0NW • 0113 214 1333*

## Skiing

**Halifax Ski Centre**
*Sportsman Leisure, Bradford Old Road, Swalesmoor, Halifax HX3 6UG • 01422 340 760*

**Harrogate Ski Centre**
*Yorkshire Showground, Hookstone, Wood Road, Harrogate HG2 8PW • 01423 505 457*

## Leisure Centres

**Aireborough Leisure Centre**
*The Green, Guiseley, Leeds LS20 9BT • 01943 877 131*
Sports hall for football, badminton and basketball, main swimming pool with diving boards and inflatable island

*Skating*

## Mini-Dipping

**You're never too young for a swim**
Babies have an innate swimming ability — hardly surprising as they've been suspended in fluid for nine months previously — and there are several classes in the region for parents wishing to help make their children feel at home in the water. Swimming is thought to improve babies' co-ordination and confidence: although it may seem scary letting go of your apparently defenceless baby in the swimming pool, babies have a natural reflex to stop them breathing in underwater, and only become scared of water if they are not used to it by around a year old. They will happily do a kind of doggy paddle underwater and can soon be taught to swim to the surface or the side of the pool — a useful first step in water safety, and they look pretty cute doing it, too.

Parent and baby sessions are on the short side — around half an hour — to stop the babies getting cold, and sessions usually take place in leisure centres' warmer small pools. Leeds Leisure Services run 'Water Babies' classes for babies from four months to four years at a wide range of leisure centres. If you can't wait that long to train your future Olympic champion, then privately-run classes will take babies that are just a few days old. These tend to be more expensive but often have smaller groups and offer the chance of having a *Nevermind*-style underwater photo taken as a souvenir of your child's watery adventures.

**Leeds Leisure Services, 0113 247 8384**
*Aireborough, Holt Park, Kippax, Middleton, Morley, Kirkstall, Rothwell, Scott Hall, South Leeds and Wetherby pools • 'Water Babies' course £51.80 (£46.20 with LeedsCard or £42.00 with Priority LeedsCard) for 14 weeks (which correspond to school terms).*

**Water Babies Swimming Club**
*Leeds Grammar School, Alwoodley Gates, Harrogate Road, Leeds • Contact Chris Jones on 0113 255 9881 for details.*

**Water Babies UK**
*6 Alexandra Crescent, Ilkley, LS29 9ER, 01943 431 490, www.swimbaby.co.uk • Classes in Ilkley, Harrogate and Leeds: lessons cost £8 each (or £7 for each additional child), bookable in blocks of five.*

*Water Babies UK*

Courtesy of Leeds Leisure Services

(weekends only), teaching pool, squash courts and climbing wall

### Armley Leisure Centre
*Carr Croft, Armley, Leeds LS12 3HB • 0113 214 3556*
Main hall, table tennis hall, swimming pool and squash courts

### Baildon Recreation Centre
*Green Lane, Baildon, BD17 5JH • 01274 599 245*
Rifle range

### Bingley Pool
*Myrtle Place, Bingley BD16 2LF • 01274 560 621*
23m x 10m swimming pool

### Boroughbridge Leisure Centre
*Wetherby Road, Boroughbridge, YO51 9HS • 01423 323 505*
Badminton courts, sports hall for netball, hockey, basketball, 5-a-side football, short tennis and table tennis. Cricket nets, squash courts, outdoor tennis courts, outdoor netball courts, astro-turf floodlit pitch, 5-a-side football, hockey, tennis and netball

### Bowling Pool
*Flockton Road, Bradford BD4 7RH • 01274 727 577*
25m x 11m swimming pool

### Bramley Baths
*Broad Lane, Leeds LS13 3DF • 0113 214 6034*
25-yard pool, with swimming lessons available

### East Leeds Leisure Centre
*Neville Road, Halton LS15 0NW • 0113 214 1333*
Sport hall, squash courts and main pool (25m x 12 m)

### Eccleshill Pool
*Harrogate Road, Bradford BD10 0QE • 01274 612 329*
33m x 13m Swimming Pool with diving area, learner pool and 20m waterslide

### Fearnville Leisure Centre
*Oakwood Lane, Leeds LS8 3LF • 0113 248 9349*
Astroturf pitch for football and hockey, junior classes in football and gymnastics, and squash courts

### Garforth Squash & Leisure Centre
*Ninelands Lane, Garforth, Leeds LS25 1NX • 0113 286 0225*
Main hall for badminton, short tennis, 5-a-side football and netball, squash courts and gymnastics coaching for both boys and girls

### Granby Community Leisure Centre
*Ainsty Road, Harrogate HG1 4AP • 01423 502 880*
Multisports session for 8-16yrs

### Grange Sports Centre
*Haycliffe Lane, Bradford BD5 9ET • 01274 572 923*
Sports hall, squash courts, athletics track, hard court area and grass pitches

### Holt Park Leisure Centre
*Holt Road, Cookridge, Leeds LS16 7QD • 0113 267 9739*
Sports hall, squash courts, teaching pool and freeform pool

### Ilkley Pool
*Denton Road, Ilkley LS29 0BZ • 01943 600 453*
25m x 10.66m swimming pool, outdoor pool and outdoor sports facilities

### John Smeaton Centre
*Smeaton Approach, Crossgates Leeds LS15 8TA • 0113 260 1853*
Sports hall for badminton, 5-a-side football, basketball and netball, 25m pool, girls and boys gym classes, junior activities, outdoor netball courts, redgra pitches, football, hockey and rugby fields

### Kippax Leisure Centre
*Station Road, Kippax, Leeds LS25 7LQ • 0113 286 8882*
Sports hall for football, basketball and badminton, and 25m x 12m pool

### Kirkstall Leisure Centre
*Kirkstall Lane, Leeds LS5 3BE • 0113 2144 556*
The main sports hall can accommodate badminton, 5-a- side football and gymnastics. Four squash courts, main pool, small pool and multi purpose activity room

### Leeds International Pool
*Westgate, Leeds LS1 4PH • 0113 214 5000*
50m Pool, learner Pool, diving pit with 3, 5, 7, 10m fixed boards and 1 and 3m springboards

### Manningham Sports Centre
*Carlisle Road, Bradford BD8 8BA • 01274 494 927*
Double sports hall, floodlit synthetic pitch and 18m x 6m swimming pool

**SKYLARK SOCCER**

Skylark Football Arenas offer the ideal venue for children's birthday parties. For football, 10-pin bowling or a combination of the two, along with food from the "Stadia Express" café a memorable party is guaranteed.

 5-A-SIDE FOOTBALL

 KIDS COACHING

 BIRTHDAY PARTIES

 10 PIN BOWLING

 STADIA EXPRESS CAFÉ

# SKYLARK SOCCER

1 Benyon Park Way, off Lowfields Road, Leeds  LS12 6DP

Tel: 0113 244 8219
Email: admin@skylarksoccer.com

*Skylark Leisure*

## Marley Activities & Coaching Centre

*Aireworth Road, Keighley BD21 4DB • 01535 609 910*
Floodlit synthetic pitch, sports hall (with synthetic floor surface), floodlit tarmac area and grass pitches

## Middleton Leisure Centre

*Ring Road, Middleton, Leeds LS10 4AX • 0113 277 0021*
Main hall used for football, badminton, netball, basketball, tennis, short tennis and martial arts. Badminton courts, outdoor football pitch, squash courts and swimming pool (18 x 7m)

## Morley Leisure Centre

*Queensway, Morley, Leeds LS27 9JP • 0113 253 6854*
Sports halls for football, netball, basketball and badminton, diving pool, squash courts, 25m pool and teaching pool. Tae Kwan Do classes, swimming lessons and life saving classes for rookies. Gymnastics lessons

## Nab Wood Sports Centre

*Cottingley, New Rd, Bingley BD16 1TZ • 01274 567 285*
Sports halls, squash courts, hard porous area, tennis, netball courts and grass pitches

## Nidderdale Recreation Centre

*Low Wath Road, Pateley Bridge, Harrogate HG3 5HL • 01423 711 442*
Gymnastics development programme for 2 year-olds upwards. Badminton courts, squash courts, outdoor tennis courts and netball courts

## Pudsey Leisure Centre

*Market Place, Leeds LS28 9JB • 0113 256 8903*
Sports hall for football, badminton, basketball, gymnastics, and full swimming programme

## Queensbury Pool

*Station Road, Queensbury BD13 1AB • 01274 883 978*
18 x 7m swimming pool, with inflatable slide during special sessions

## Rhodesway Pool

*Oaks Lane, Bradford BD15 7RU • 01274 495481*
25 x 10m swimming pool

## Richard Dunn Sports Centre

*Rooley Avenue, Odsal BD6 1EZ • 01274 307 822*
Squash courts, floodlit hard porous area and swimming pool with 'cobra' black hole waterslide and 'zambezee' tyre ride

## Ripon Leisure Centre

*Dallamires Lane, Ripon HG4 1TT • 01765 601 353*
Sports hall, badminton courts and sports coaching courses

## Rossett Sports Centre

*Pannal Ash Road, Harrogate HG2 9JP • 01423 505 455*
Tennis courts, archery courses for juniors, cricket course for 7-11 yrs, sports hall, squash courts, synthetic pitch, netball/tennis courts

## Rothwell Leisure Centre

*Wakefield Road, Oulton Leeds LS26 8EL • 0113 282 4110*
Sports hall for badminton, 5-a-side football, gymnastics, karate and judo. 25 x 12.5m pool, teaching pool and swimming lessons.

## Scott Hall Leisure Centre

*Scott Hall Road, Leeds LS7 3DT • 0113 262 3942*
Sports hall for football, badminton, basketball, gymnastics and short tennis. Pool offers largest

swimming lesson programme in the city, including water safety.

### Scotchman Road Activities & Coaching Centre
*Scotchman Road, Bradford BD9 5AT • 01274 544 389*
Synthetic pitch, tarmac area

### Shipley Pool
*Alexandra Road, Shipley BD18 3ER • 01274 437 162*
25 x 13m swimming pool with diving pool and teaching pool

### South Leeds Sports Centre
*Beeston Road, Leeds LS11 6TP • 0113 245 7549*
Main hall and outdoor court for football, netball, badminton, basketball and tennis. Squash courts, small pool, main pool with pool inflatables, and private swimming lessons

### The Leisure Centre Keighley
*Victoria Park, Keighley BD21 3JN • 01535 681 763*
Sports Hall, Squash Courts and Leisure Pool with 40m waterslide and plunge pool learner pool

### Thornton Recreation Centre
*Leaventhorpe Lane, Bradford BD13 3BH • 01274 883 874*
Sports hall and synthetic pitch

### Tong Recreation Centre & Pool
*Westgate Hill, Bradford BD4 6NR • 01274 683 922*
Sports hall and 23m x 9m swimming pool

### Wetherby Leisure Centre
*The Ings, Boston Road, Wetherby, Leeds LS22 5HA • 01937 585 125*
25m main pool and learner pool. Runs a rookie lifeguard class on a Saturday morning and Monday evenings for young lifeguards

## Sports to Watch
The only chance of live summer sport used to be having to sit in front of the box watching England's cricketers getting walloped or seeing how many British players could reach the second week at Wimbledon. Not any more, thankfully (though still possible to do).

### Bradford Bulls
The legendary Odsal stadium comes into its own during those hot early-evening kick-offs.
*Odsal Stadium, Bradford, BD6 1BS • 08701 202 040 • Adults from £12, Children from £6, Family ticket (one adult, two children) from £18*

### Bradford City
With the season kick-off now in early August, you can now suffer home-match heartbreak in sultry conditions too.
*Valley Parade, Burlington Street, Bradford, BD8 7EG • 01274 770 022 • Adults start at £15, Children £5, Family ticket (one adult, two children) £19*

### Castleford Tigers
The Tigers are looking to make home advantage count in a push for a shock top-four finish this season.

Headingley Cricket Ground

Wheldon Road, Castleford, WF10 2SD • 01977 552
674

### Halifax Town
About the cheapest seats to watch football in the area
Shay Stadium, Shaw Hill, Halifax, HX1 2YT • 01422
349 438 • Adults £10, Children £5

### Horsforth Hall Park Cricket Club
The perfect place to spend Sunday afternoons
Hall Park, Ring Rd, Leeds, LS18 4EL • 0113 258 6859

### Huddersfield Giants
Not having a great time of it recently, but at least you
get to experience a great stadium ...
The Alfred McAlpine Stadium, Stadium Way, Leeds Road,
Huddersfield, HD1 6PZ • 01484 530 710 • Adults
from £14, Children from £7

### Huddersfield Town
... with the same being said for the football team too.
The Alfred McAlpine Stadium, Stadium Way, Leeds Road,
Huddersfield, HD1 6PZ • 01484 484 100 • Adults
from £14, Children from £7

### Kinsley Greyhound Stadium
The dogs are open Tuesday, Friday and Saturday nights.
96 Wakefield Rd, Kinsley, Pontefract, WF9 5EH •
01977 610 946 • Adults from £4, 14-16 year olds £3,
8-13 year olds £1, under 8 free

### Leeds Rhinos
Serious contenders for the Grand Final at last? Only
one way to find out.
Headingley Stadium, Leeds, LS6 3BU • 0113 2786 181
• Adults start at £15, Children £5

### Leeds United
Find out who's out and who's also out at Elland Road
with an early Premiership start in mid-August.
Elland Road, Leeds, LS11 0ES • 0113 367 6000 •
Adults from £20, Children from £14, Family ticket (two
adults, two children) from £55

### Pontefract Park Race Course
Free entry at the race tracks makes for a cheap and
enjoyable day out
Pontefract Park, Pontefract, WF8 4RA • 01977 702 210
• Adults from £3, Kids (under 16) free

### Wetherby Racecourse
York Rd, Wetherby, LS22 5EJ • 01937 582 035 • Adults
from £3, Kids (under 16) free

### Yorkshire County Cricket Club
County matches, an England Test Match and a One
Day International means a busy summer for
Headingley.
Headingley Cricket Ground, Leeds, LS6 3BU • (0113)
278 7394 • Adults from £22, Kids from £11 (for inter-
national matches)

Leeds Rhino's

Parties & Playtime

*Bob's Your Uncle*

Have the kids stopped being impressed by your jokes? Do you blanch at the thought of trying to entertain all of their mates? Here are some ideas for parties that will be memorable for all the *right* reasons.

## Party Venues

### 1st Choice Childrens Discos
Fun, games, bubbles, classic party games & competitions for five-10 year-olds • Chart music, lights & smoke for 11-17 year-olds
*42 Woodside Dv, Cottingley, Bingley* • *01274 561 902* • *Ages 5-17*

### Ace Crazy Karting
*9 Spring Holes Lane, Thornton, Bradford* • *01274 742556* • *Capacity 40*

### AMF Bowling
*Leeds Bowl, Merrion Centre, Merrion Way, Leeds* • *0113 245 1781*

### Childrens paintball command
Army style action • Challenges and games, paintball shooting tuition • Camouflage uniforms provided, activity certificates for each child

*Castle Farm, Milnthorpe Lane, Wakefield* • *0808 108 9831* • *Ages 5-14*

### Hollywood Bowl
*The Leisure Exchange, Vicar Lane, Bradford* • *01274 734 222*

### LA Bowl
Bowling or quasar • Prices include one hour of bowling, game of quasar (30-minute session, including a 10-minute brief, 15-minute game and five-minute de-brief) or one session of dodgems • Meal, soft drinks, ice cream, party bag and gift for the birthday child included in price
*Sweet Street, Holbeck, Leeds* • *0113 242 1330* • *Children £7-£7.50*

### Monkey Maze
Themed party rooms — choose from Pooh's Picnic Corner, Under the Sea, Cartoon Room and Never Never Land • Hot and cold food served as part of the party • Price includes party bag and balloon
*Ninelands Lane, Garforth, East Garforth, Leeds* • *0113 287 2766* • *Open Daily 10am-7pm, Visit time 1 hour* • *Children £5.75*

### Polly Paintpot and Honey Bear
Puppets and crazy balloon creations
*135 Ring Road, Lower Wortley, Leeds* • *0113 263 9722*

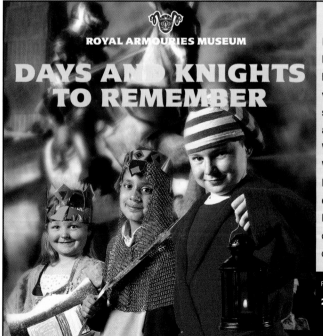

**ROYAL ARMOURIES MUSEUM**

**DAYS AND KNIGHTS TO REMEMBER**

Imagine if you could invite King Henry VIII to your birthday party, craft your very own suit of armour, or sleepover in a gallery with all the knights and armour! Wouldn't it be amazing? Well, there's more to the Royal Armouries than you could ever have imagined! For more information on all our childrens activities, just call our information line.

Royal Armouries Museum, Armouries Drive, Leeds, LS10 1LT
**24 Hour Information Line**
**0113 220 1999**
Internet: www.armouries.org.uk.
Email: enquiries@armouries.org.uk.

### Pro Am Indoor Karting

Full circuit and mini races • Mixed ages not a problem • Four karts per race • Party invites and certificates for all drivers • £99 for one hour
*Bawtry Road, Selby • 01757 213 636 • Open Midweek, Sat-Sun, Ages 4-10*

### Wild Wild West

Choice of hot meal and ice lolly for dessert and unlimited drink in own party room • Price includes party invitations, gift bags & parking • Toddlers' parties for under-threes • Whole venue can be hired for £99
*York Road, Leeds • 0113 217 4444 • Visit time 2 hours • Children £4-£6*

### York Megabowl

*Clifton Moor Centre, Stirling Road, York • 01904 690006*

## Entertainers

### A Kind of Magic

Balloons, puppets & magician
*29 Croft House grove, Morely, Leeds • 0113 253 5289*

### Aardvark Castles Ltd

Bouncy castles, funhouses, gladiators, slides
*36 Primley Park Mount, Leeds • 0113 269 1229 • Ages test, Visit time test*

### Altered Ego

*25 Wadehouse Avenue, Shelf, Halifax • 01274 674 692*

### Art Cart

*1 Hollin Hall Farm, Long Causeway, Denholme, Bradford • 01274 833 978*

### B2 Faced Face Painting

*12 Hawkswood Road, Horsforth, Leeds • 0113 258 7133*

### Bobs your Uncle

Fun, magic, games & competitions • Puppet and magic shows for young children • Action magic discos for older children
*The Magic Cherry Tree Cottage, Copgrove, Harrogate • 01423 340 568*

### Boos disco

*2 Lickless Terrace, Horsforth, Leeds • 0113 230 1110*

### Daniels Disco

*PO Box 4, Leeds • 07071 289 289*

## STER CENTURY
### CINEMAS

## IT'S THE ULTIMATE
## KIDS CINEMA EXPERIENCE
Ster Century Cinemas in Leeds presents the best action-packed day out in town.

★★★★★★★★★★★★★★★★★★★★★★★★

### KIDS PARTIES
Just look at what they get:
• Kids combo snack • Group Photo • Presents • Games • giant carpeted Snakes & Ladders board
Plus
Watching a film on the biggest screens, with the best sound and the comfiest seats
All this for only £7 per head or £7.50 for bookings after september 1st 2003

★★★★★★★★★★★★★★★★★★★★★★

### KIDS CLUB
Every Saturday and Sunday morning at approx. 11.00am (or every day during school holidays)

Only £1 per ticket

★★★★★★★★★★★★★★★★★★★★★★
And there's a wide range of snacks available
• Freshly popped popcorn • Hot and cold drinks • Hot Dogs • Nachos • Sweets • Ben and Jerry's Ice Cream!

### Kid's Combo Meal
Regular popcorn, Drink and sweets - all for just £3.50
★★★★★★★★★★★★★★★★★★★★★★
For further details about children's parties or the Kid's Club contract

## PHILIPPA COLE ON
## 0113 224 0581

**STER CENTURY CINEMAS**
The Light on the Headrow in Leeds
Box office 0870 240 3696
www.stercentury.co.uk

## Birthday Parties

Fancy a birthday party with a difference? Then The Royal Armouries Museum is the perfect venue: 4 to 12 year-olds can celebrate in style and more importantly, impress their friends at the same time! Parties cost just £6.95 per child (minimum of six children) and include a special guided tour of the museum, a great chance to see some of the most interesting pieces in the collection and hear the fascinating stories behind the objects. Lunch is followed by hands-on creative activities, plus a goody bag to take home.

## Sleepovers

Themed around special events in the museum or to mark occasions such as Halloween or Christmas, sleepovers are great fun and very popular with children and adults alike! Enjoy a range of organised activities including games, storytelling and dancing followed by a treasure trail. When morning comes, a hot breakfast is a welcome start to the day. Our sleepovers are ideal for families, and larger groups (minimum 50) can have their very own tailor-made evening. Prices are £13/child or £6/adults.

## Artkart Activities

An ideal opportunity for kids to make something which they can take home with them. Whether it's a sword or shield, armour, embossed copper designs or a clay model, imaginations can run wild. The Artkart runs at weekends and every day during school holidays. Families can drop in whilst larger groups can book in advance. A small charge of £1-£2 applies.

**For further details of all these call the 24-hour info line on 0113 229 1999.**

### Fairy Parties
*28 Parish Ghyll Road, Ilkley • 01943 605091*

### Fancy Cats and Arts Attack Workshop
Face Painting by Fancy Cats is a professional face paint team and Arts Attack Workshop will do fancy hair braids and glitter hair colour
*17 Summerhill Road, Leeds • 0113 2860626*

### The Great Si Mona
*80 Fair Road, Bradford • 01274 408806*

### Henrietta Rabbit Childrens Entertainer
*The Warren, Eden Close, York • 0800 0965653*

### Kiddies Castles
*30 Burley Avenue, Killinghall, Harrogate • 01423 526678*

### Myster Yaffe
Comedy, magic, puppets, ventriloquism
*422 Street Lane, Leeds • 0113 288 8053*

### SAS Bouncy Castle Hire
Bouncy castles, ball pools, gladiators, slides, activity bouncers, obstacle courses, garden games, rodeo bull and surf simulator, electric carts
*Sommerdale Gardens, Leeds • 0113 257 1901*

### Shaunas Bouncers
Themed bouncy castles
*19 Asket Avenue, Leeds • 0113 2650 498*

### Truffles the Clown
Magic, games, balloon modelling, music, juggling & life-size teddy bears who dance with the children
*13 East Moor Crescent, Roundhay, Leeds • 0113 266 5526*

## Adventure Playgrounds

### Adventure World
*Unit 2, James Street, Elland • 01422 252208 • Students £1*

### Alphabet Zoo
Play centre, singing, dancing, kids' characters
*Unit 4, Four Lanes Business Park, Cemetery Road, Bradford • 01274 788 883 •*
*Thornes Lane, Wakefield • 01924 299 898*

### Jimmy Gs Adventure Zone
*Saltaire Roundabout, Bradford • 01274 533 848*

### Scallywags playgym
Climbing frames, rockers, Wendy house, bouncy castles and ball pool • Parties at weekends
*280 Whingate Junction, Leeds • 0113 231 9344 • Ages 0-6*

Days Out

Leeds-Liverpool Canal, Saltaire

With coast, countryside and other cities all within 90 minutes' travel and a relatively efficient public transport system, Yorkshire has countless destinations that it's worth packing the sandwiches for. If you can bear the cries of 'Are we there yet?' five minutes after leaving home, trips to these places should keep even the most holiday-jaded youngster amused.

## The Deep

A train to Hull will bring you within easy reach of The Deep, the region's very best 'World Ocean Discovery Centre'. (You may have seen the staff mucking about in the advert for the latest national Lottery scratchcard.)

Outside, the tetrahedral-shaped complex juts out over the River Humber impressively. Inside, it houses the deepest tank and viewing tunnel in the world, as well as numerous exhibits illustrating the changes in the underwater world since the dawn of time. Not only does it mean no weather-related worrying, you can also spend the day gawping at a variety of exotic aquatic life-forms like the centre's new Grey Reef Sharks (a UK first) or immerse yourself in the wonders of the Amazon River Basin courtesy of Deep Blue One, a futuristic deep-sea research station. Little monsters will be pleased to know there are tonnes of interactive multi-media activities (ie computer games) for them to tinker with too.

The Deep is within walking distance of Hull city centre, and the number 90 bus will get you from the train station to the site. If you're driving, there is a car-park on site which costs £3 (£2 of which is redeemable against purchases in the shop or cafe).
Hull, HU1 4DP • 01482 381000 • www.thedeep.co.uk

## Filey

Scarborough's smaller and less hectic cousin. Filey offers sandy beaches with plenty of shells, teeming rockpools and beautiful views from the windswept Filey Brigg, which jutts out into the sea. The town has a traditional seaside feel, with plenty of teeth-rotting rock available to make little hands sticky.

## Scarborough

Everything a family resort should be, Scarborough has sandy beaches (although the chilly North Sea is an acquired taste), seafront walks and plenty of garish tack to keep little ones amused. The South Bay is the busier of the two, with chipshops, amusement arcades and stalls selling candyfloss and cups of winkles: marvel at the shiny (working) lifeboat which is poised for action

The Deep

or make yourself giddy on the fairground rides. Meanwhile the North Bay is quieter, with more space to build sandcastles: its most striking landmark is the collection of white pyramids that make up the sea life centre, whose residents include seahorses and rescued seals. Scarborough's other attractions include an outdoor aquapark for those not wishing to brave the sea, and the castle, whose ruins are brought to life with an audiotour and which is well worth climbing the steep path up to the clifftop to visit.

## Ilkley

Though Ilkley itself is a bit too twee and self-important to provide much fun for children, its famous moor provides all the entertainment an energetic youngster could want. The famous Cow and Calf Rocks provide some excellent amateur climbing opportunities (though it is of course essential that parents keep a close eye on things — getting up tends not to be a problem, it's the getting down that the fire brigade frequently have to help out with). Ilkely's one concession to run-around fun is a good one: the lido, a lagoon-shaped outdoor pool with diving area and fountain.

Saltaire

## Saltaire

If you want to enjoy a side helping of history with your day out, Saltaire is a good choice. The focal point of the village, Salts Mill, was built by the philanthropist Sir Titus Salt in the 19th century, and the gridwork of streets that stretch from it housed his workers. Today the giant mill machinery has gone, replaced with shops, galleries and a restaurant. Children who appreciate art

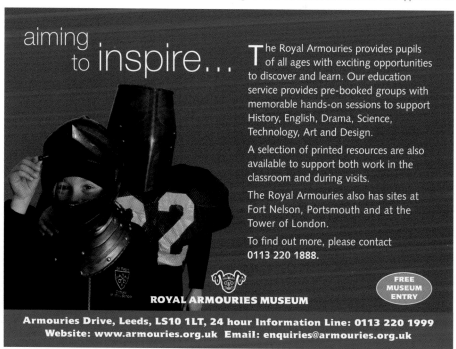

aiming
to inspire...

The Royal Armouries provides pupils of all ages with exciting opportunities to discover and learn. Our education service provides pre-booked groups with memorable hands-on sessions to support History, English, Drama, Science, Technology, Art and Design.

A selection of printed resources are also available to support both work in the classroom and during visits.

The Royal Armouries also has sites at Fort Nelson, Portsmouth and at the Tower of London.

To find out more, please contact **0113 220 1888.**

**ROYAL ARMOURIES MUSEUM**

FREE MUSEUM ENTRY

**Armouries Drive, Leeds, LS10 1LT, 24 hour Information Line: 0113 220 1999
Website: www.armouries.org.uk  Email: enquiries@armouries.org.uk**

## Canals and Waterways

Relaxing, educational and with plenty of nature and slimy things to spot ... canals are your route to a great day out

### Huddersfield Canal

Since the renovation of the Huddersfield Canal, giant steps have been taken to improve both access to and enjoyment of this great British treasure. At over three and a half miles long, the famous Standedge Tunnel is the highest, longest and deepest canal tunnel in Britain and the recently opened Standedge Visitors' Centre runs regular guided day trips through it. There is also a gift shop and interactive resource centre as well as a licensed restaurant.

*Standedge Visitors' Centre, Waters Road, Marsden, Huddersfield • 01484 844 298*

### Rochdale Canal

Barge Branwell is a converted motor barge, last used to carry 60 tonnes of coal to Dewsbury Power Station. It has been brought to Hebden Bridge and restored with a traditional boatman's cabin and small exhibition. Admission is free and there are ice-creams and sweets available once inside, if you can move enough to get your purse open. Traditional horse-drawn and motorboat cruises are also available Easter to Christmas for groups and individuals.

*Barge Branwell Visitor Centre, Hebden Bridge Marina • 01422 845 557*

### River Ouse

The River Ouse used to be the main waterway to York from the Humber and North Sea, providing the main access to the city for the Vikings and Romans. Nowadays it is principally used for recreational purposes and the odd Viking re-enactment. Yorkboat operate nightly 'ghost cruises' as well as themed, 'Disco', 'Caribbean' and 'Jazz' cruises.

*YorkBoat, The Boatyard, Lendal Bridge, York • 01904 628 324*

### Leeds-Liverpool Canal

The Leeds-Liverpool canal is West Yorkshire's oldest and the only trans-Pennine canal still fully open to navigation. Apollo Canal Cruises run regular day trips along the canal with several stopping points on the way so you can join halfway through, eventually finishing at the famous Five Rise Lock at Bingley, so named because there are five very steeply rising locks in close proximity.

*Apollo Canal Cruises, Wharf Street, Shipley • 01274 595 914*

Standedge Tunnel Visitor Centre, Marsden

Photo courtesy of British Waterways

will enjoy the vast collection of work by local lad David Hockney, but for those that don't there's a generously stocked children's bookshop. A short walk up Victoria Road will take you to the Reed Organ and Harmonium Museum, one of only two in Europe exclusively devoted to the Reed Organ and Harmonium. Owners Phil and Pam Fluke will personally lead you around their collection. More energetic but equally historic fun can be had on Shipley Glen Cable Tramway, the oldest working cable tramway in Great Britain. From the top station, it's a short walk to the Children's Funfair & Pleasure Grounds — itself with over a century of tradition. Saltaire is also bisected by the Leeds-Liverpool canal, and a regular waterbus will take you to the impressive five rise locks in Bingley.

## Whitby

An ancient fishing port that nestles between the North Yorks Moors and the North Sea at the mouth of the River Esk, Whitby is most famous as the place where Dracula washed up after his trip from Transylvania. On a windswept day you can certainly see what inspired Bram Stoker as the ruins of St Hilda's Abbey high on the East Cliff bear down on the village and the maze of alleyways and narrow streets by the quayside offer

plenty of nooks and crannies for spectral transformations. But on brighter days it takes on a more benign personality and is a picturesque place to take in some briney air.

## Bridlington

A traditional-style seaside resort with a hefty dose of nostalgia, Bridlington offers plenty to see even if you're allergic to sand. Tour around the John Bull confectionery factory to see how traditional favourites such as toffee and seaside rock are made or take a one-hour cruise on the Yorkshire Belle boat. Bridlington even has a museum devoted to visiting the seaside: at the 'Beside the Seaside' museum, kids can sit in a Victorian Rail carriage, 'experience' a 50s boarding house and have a go at running a Punch and Judy show. Elsewhere in the town, the retro-styled Sixties Coffee Bar offers refreshments and memorabilia: the younger generation will probably be eager to head upstairs to Old Penny Memories, a museum of antique slot machines in working order.

## Sheffield

Although it still bears the scars of a bad encounter with 60s architecture and has a worryingly large amount of

Filey

A fantastic and memorable day out awaits at The Royal Armouries Museum! Over 8000 exhibits are displayed in five themed galleries: War, Tournament, Oriental, Hunting and Self Defence. History is brought to life both inside and outside the museum by highly-trained interpreters in full replica costume who describe the dramatic, harrowing and perilous stories of people whose lives were touched by the objects on display, including experiences from The Battle of Hastings to the dressing of a Samurai Warrior, armed combat demonstrations with swords and pollaxes through to more recent day conflict such as the Great War, Vietnam and Bosnia. whilst the armed combat demonstrations include fighting with swords and pollaxes.

Specially themed events provide visitors with the chance to take an in-depth look at history. Events take place during school holidays with something for the entire family, ranging from children's activities, interpretations, demonstrations, story-telling to horse-shows, lectures, films, family trails and tours.

The Tiltyard seats 1200 people: from April to October (weather permitting) this is where you can see the Royal Armouries horses and riders: experience the sounds of pounding hooves, the clash of lances, cries, cheers and applause from the audience. See the resident falconer fly his beautiful, graceful birds of prey or visit the armourers' workshop.

An exciting events programme is planned for 2003/2004: ring the information line on 0113 220 1999 for further details or go to www.armouries.org.uk. You'll be inspired to visit again and again as every day at the Royal Armouries is unique and what's more... it's FREE!

Huddersfield Canal

Photo courtesy of British Waterways

pound shops, Sheffield is hot on Leeds' heels in the regeneration race. The newest and most spectacular of these projects is the Winter Gardens, a city-centre greenhouse — large enough to fit 5,000 normal garden greenhouses into — containing 150 species of plants from all over the world and hosting free Sunday concerts throughout summer. The Peace Gardens, despite containing some mushroom-cloud-shaped fountains of questionable taste, are a central square with a bustling, family feel to it, whilst the Millennium Galleries are a large art gallery designed to appeal to all ages.

## Skipton

Often called 'The Gateway to the Dales', Skipton is worth more than a pause to don your wellies before heading for the hills. Its castle is impressive (see the Houses and Castles section for details); the Leeds-Liverpool canal passes through whilst the town is near to the steam-engine-running Embsay and Bolton Abbey Railway (see Railways section). As a small lively town, it's lively and welcoming, making efforts to attract tourists with events such as Sheep Day and the Festival of Speed, a hair-raising soapbox race down steep hills.

# Win Family Tickets to Magna!

Magna Science Adventure Centre is a day out with something to entertain and educate the entire family. Based within the former Templeborough steelworks building in Rotherham, the centre has been given a futuristic makeover to make it into an interactive exploration of science and the elements. Within a building which still contains features from the local steel industry such as hulking hooks, cranes and winding passages, you'll find innovative technology, daring architecture and engaging interactive games and challenges.

Its five gadget-packed pavilions are themed around the elements earth, air, fire, water and power, linked by suspended walkways, scissor lifts, stairs and tunnels. Highlights include The Air Pavilion — a giant suspended 'zeppelin' — the Fire Pavilion's five-metre fire tornado; real-life JCBs to control and a quarry to explode in the subterranean Earth Pavilion; an underground tunnel leading to the Power Pavilion, where visitors can try out a giant hamster wheel and a self-lifting chair; and the splashy delights of the Water Pavilion, including a water cannon, a huge steel water wheel and overhead raining clouds.

In addition, two multimedia shows bring to life the centre's past as the workplace of 10,000 steelworkers. At 100 feet high, 'The Face Of Steel' is the largest multi-media display in the UK, whilst 'The Big Melt' recreates the steel making process in an impressive pyrotechnic and audio display.

Visitors can also marvel while taking refreshments at Magna's inflatable café — which was designed by Per Lindstrand, of Richard Branson balloon fame — whilst kids can mess around to their heart's content in the centre's adventure playground.

Opened April 2001, Magna currently has a visitor total of over 630,000 per year and has won many awards for both its architecture and as a visitor attraction.

We have ten family tickets worth £26 each to give away — these entitle up to five people (two adults and three kids) to free entry to Magna for a day.

To enter, simply send your name, address and daytime telephone number to Leeds Guide Kids Guide Competition, 30-34 Aire Street, Leeds LS1 4HT. The closing date is 30 June 2004 but the ten tickets are allocated on a first come, first-served basis, so be quick!

## Calendar of the Year 2003-4

**Don't miss these events coming up**

### July

Party in the Park (20 Jul)
Rhythms of the City (17 Jul-16 Aug)
Keighley Children's Festival (18 Jul-16 Aug)

### August

FEVA festival, Knaresborough (8-17 Aug)
Chapeltown Carnival, Leeds (Bank Holiday weekend)
Basketball Barmy in Centenary Square, Bradford
Scarecrow Festival, Kettlewell, West Yorkshire (9-17 Aug)

### September

York festival of Traditional Dance (6-7 Sep)
Victorian Funfair, Centenary Square, Bradford

### October

Ilkley Literature Festival: Kids' weekend with Jacqueline Wilson and Ben Zephaniah (10-12 Oct)
Steam Gala Weekend, Bradford

### November

BAF! — Bradford Animation Festival, NMPFT
Christmas Market in Leeds (27 Nov-21 Dec)
Children's Christmas Fair in York (throughout Nov and Dec)

### December

Christmas Lights switch-on, Leeds
Christmas market in Bradford
Santa Specials on the Keighley and Worth Valley Train
New Year's Eve family event, Millennium Square, Leeds

### January 2004

Ice Cube, Millennium Square, Leeds, (16 Jan-29 Feb)

### February

Valentine's funfair, Leeds

## March

Childrens' Film Festival, Leeds

## April

Fete des Fleurs, Millennium Square, Leeds
International Youth Music Festival, Harrogate

## May

Fashion show, Briggate, Leeds
Ilkley Carnival, Ilkley

## June

Bradford Festival, Bradford

## Royal Armouries: The Year Ahead

**19 July-31 August: Summer of Sport**
Six weeks of activities based on sporting themes kicking off with the first ever North of England skill-at-arms competition, plus demonstrations of fencing, archery, martial arts and over the August Bank Holiday the prestigious jousting tournament for the Queens Trophy. Visitors will also get the chance to "have a go" at Fencing and Archery in specially run sessions — you may be a natural.

**25 October-2 November: Renegades**
Gain an insight into the shady lives of some of history's most infamous outlaws. An interpretation-led event with lots of activities both inside and outside the museum.

**November: A month of Remembrance**
During November the Armouries honours the memory of those who lost their lives in the service of their country including the supporting roles of those on the home front.

**20 December-4 January 2004: Global Christmas**
A closer look at different cultures around the world and how they celebrate Christmas. There will be storytelling, puppet shows, interpretations, films and lots more!

**January 2004-December 2004**
A full programme of events for 2004 will be available towards the end of this year. For a copy of the programme or for further details on any of the above events then please call the 24-hour information line on 0113 220 1999 or email : enquiries@armouries.org.uk. Details of all events are also available at www.armouries.org.uk.

## Travel Info

**Are we there yet?**

West Yorkshire is fortunate in having a comprehensive and relatively cheap public transport system, with the Metrozone of subsidised train fares stretching out as far as Walsden — that's virtually Manchester! Things get a little more pricey if you want to head north, as Harrogate, York and the Yorkshire Dales are in another travel zone. But kids — under 16s on trains, under-14s or under-18s in full-time education on buses — travel for half price on most services, and there are numerous special offers and further discounts available.

**The New School Plus MetroCard -just the ticket**

**M** wymetro.com

From August for all full time school students aged 5 - 18. Visit our web site at www.wymetro.com or call MetroLine on 0113 245 7676 for details

Metro. Here to get you there

## Buses

Unsurprisingly buses tend to be concentrated in the region's more urban areas, with services dropping off sharply towards areas such as the Yorkshire Dales, however the majority of places are reachable with some degree of planning. Many buses now have pushchair-friendly features such as alcoves at the front and lowering floors. Bus company First offers travel for just £1 throughout West Yorkshire for kids during school holidays.

## Trains

Family railcards cost £20 for a year and are valid on all networks, although not necessarily at all times of day. They give a discount of a third on adult fares and 60% on children's fares and can be used for groups of up to four adults and four children. Look out for tickets such as Metro DayRovers as well, which can be used on both buses and trains and cost from just £6 for a day's travel for up to five people.

## Cycling

Although West Yorkshire has its share of cycle lanes, you may feel unhappy about letting your kids use ones which run next to busy roads. A good alternative for a family day out is to use the network of canal towpaths: many restoration projects have been carried out recently to make sure the paths are smooth and uncluttered, and the routes are generally flat. You will need a cycling permit for each rider which costs £2 per year, available from British Waterways.

**Metroline: 0113 245 7676 • www.wymetro.com**
For public transport information in West Yorkshire.

**National Rail Enquiries: 08457 48 49 50 • www.nationalrail.co.uk**
For train times and fares nationally.

# Metro Train Map

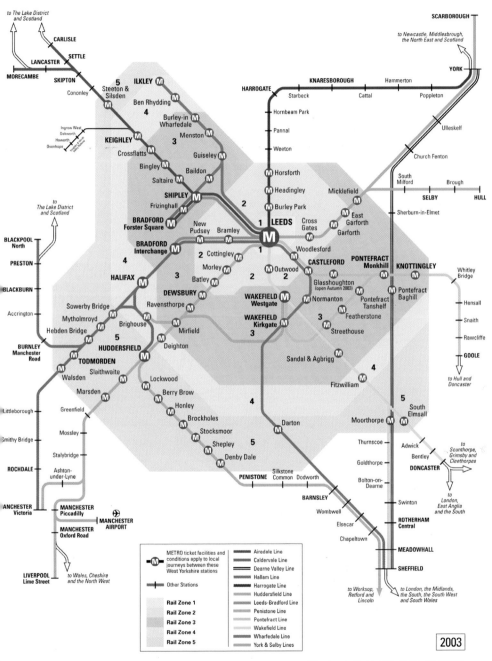

Bradford

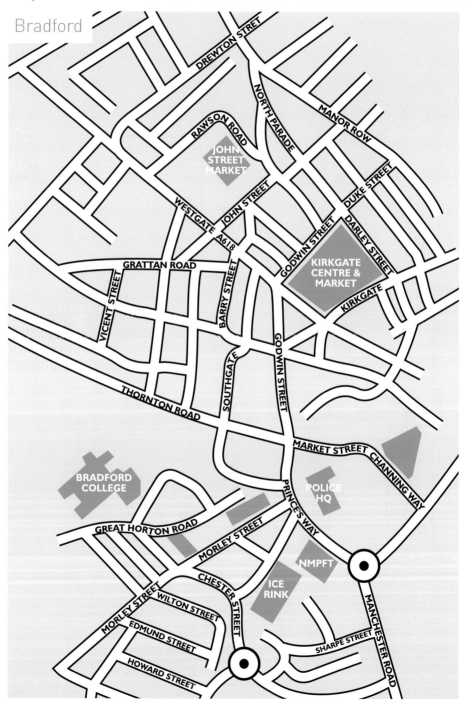

## Harrogate

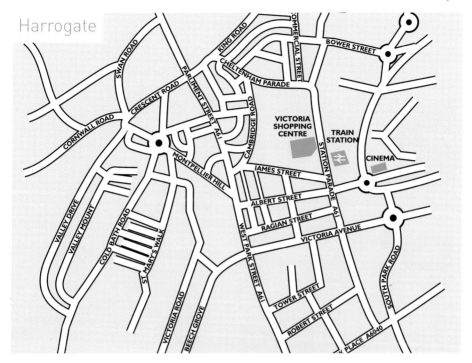

## Road Map

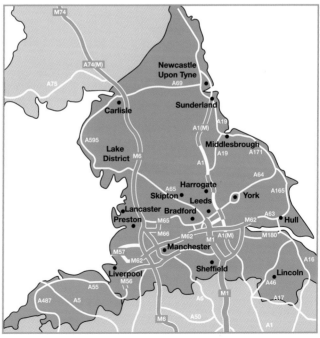

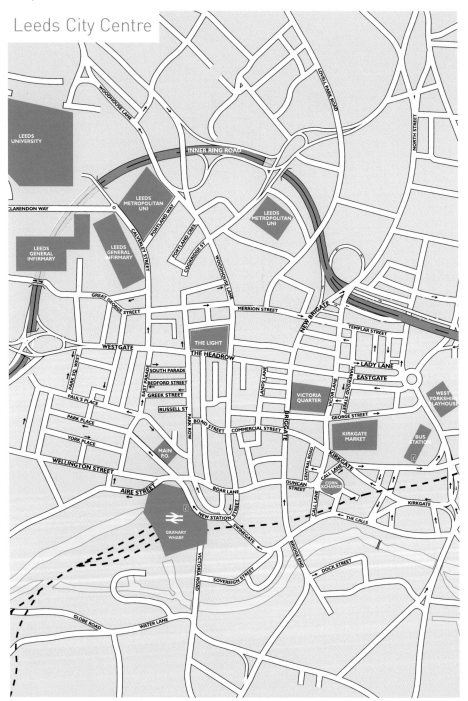

Leeds City Centre

# Index